15.89

The Perfect Galley Book

For my mother, whose
untamed and unquenchable spirit
set me to thinking

DIANE TAYLOR

The
Perfect
Galley
Book

YARNS, RECIPES & TIPS FROM
THE HEART OF THE SHIP

illustrated by John Visser

New York · Toronto · Munich

A New Trend Book
New York, Toronto, Munich

Published by
New Trend Publishers
31 Portland Street
Toronto, Ontario M5V 2V9

Distributed in the United States by
Dodd, Mead & Company
79 Madison Avenue
New York, N.Y. 10016

Library of Congress Catalog Card Number: 83-61959

Canadian Cataloguing in Publication Data

Taylor, Diane.
    The perfect galley book

ISBN 0-88639-007-9

1. Galleys (Ship kitchens).   2. Cookery, Marine.   3. Sea
stories.   4. Sailing.   I. Title.

VK224.T39   1983   641.5'753   C83-098859-6

Printed and bound in Canada

CONTENTS

PART IV

Introduction

My husband, Gary Hodgkins, and I have been nosing around boats, cooking on the watery main and designing galleys for various vessels for twelve years. We've had two boats of our own: *Isla*, the 46' trimaran that we built from scratch and lost on a reef after sailing her for three years; and *Mariposa*, the 29' trimaran that we rebuilt from a derelict and which still hobs at anchor outside our house in the Turks and Caicos Islands. We have both worked, crewed and cooked on a number of multihulls and monohulls.

The Hodgkins family and the Taylor family moved to the same small farming town in the same year, 1953. The result was that Gary and I went through the local high school, which then boasted an enrolment of 250, together. We dated off and on, mostly off. I left town after high school and trained as a medical laboratory technician, took a B.A. at university, and taught French and physical education in high schools for five years. Gary trained himself as a commercial artist, and had a successful business in this field.

Gary and I hadn't seen each other since school days when we got the feeling that we might work something out. He rang me up and told me he'd already started an outrigger. And from that time on, Gary and I and boats have been inseparable.

It struck us, after we'd been building *Isla* for a year or so, that we ought to do some extensive sailing. It would be rather silly to finish the boat and find out *then* that we hated sailing, or were perpetually seasick, or any one of a number of dreadful unknowns. It was at that point, in 1973, that we took a winter off to sail the Pacific on *La Paz*. We launched *Isla* the following year and, as I mentioned, came to grief in 1977. Pursuing several boat-related activities, (Gary, carpentry; me, upholstery), we eventually saved enough to buy the forlorn little *Mariposa*. She deposited us on the shores of Pice Cay in the Turks and Caicos Islands in May of 1980, and it must have been a fascinating island, because we're still there. Gary is manager of PRIDE, a nonprofit organization that is attempting to preserve the ecology of the islands, and to decrease the island's dependency on the mainland. PRIDE has a conch mariculture program, and does research in wind and solar energy.

But this job of his *does* cut into our sailing time. It may have to go.

Preface

Tug boat, fishing smack, tall ships and small. Cargo craft, sailing barge, super tanker, ice breaker, and pleasure-seeking ocean liner. The dhow, the curragh, the junk. Phoenician horse-headed trading vessel, and Polynesian voyaging canoe. *Titanic. Ra. Bluenose. L'Hérétique. Moxie. Spray.*

All have plied the waters of the world. Thousands of men and women have travelled millions of miles, carrying a wondrous assortment of foods and goods, lore and lies, down river, down island, and across the sea. If all their stories had been recorded, it would take more than a lifetime to read them.

And an intrinsic part of all these boats, and all these adventures, has been the galley.

* * *

Sailors are of a nomadic breed. The weekender thrills to put miles under the hull, and quietly rejoices when evidence of the maddening crowd recedes into the mist over the stern. The cruiser calls no place home, and yet is happily at home everywhere.

Whether short or long-distance sailors, almost all will agree that food assumes a far greater significance on board than it ever does on land. The galley is always alive — it doesn't shift gears into neutral, as does the rest of the ship, when the anchor takes. When members of the crew retire below to rest from reefing in the gale, they are always cheered when greeted by good smells from the galley. And it is at the table with the warmth of food in the stomach and the warmth of camaraderie in the air that much of the yarning goes on.

In the days before ships carried a medical crew, the cook (often dubbed "doctor") was in charge of the medicine chest, and again today on many small boats it is usually the cook, with his or her bits of knowledge on sterilization, water purification and nutrition, who fills this role. Frequently, it is also the cook who takes responsibility for preparing the survival bucket. And it is generally the cook who takes an individual interest in the crew, and to whom the crew looks for fun and affection.

And, of course, there's nothing like food when you're hungry.

For all these reasons, the galley is often referred to as, and in fact often is, *the heart of the ship.*

PART I
"This Sailing's the Life"

It is curious how sometimes a path you trod briefly and gracelessly as a child, simply because you were dragged forcibly along, may later become the focus of your entire life.

The "pleasure" cruise I took with my family at the age of fourteen is a case in point. We hated it. All of us. Except father, of course — it was his idea. There we were, the four of us, — mother, father, two girls — spending a three-week vacation on a cabin cruiser that slept two. Father was in exuberant good spirits (as usual) telling us every five minutes what a marvellous time we were all having. He didn't seem to notice that his three women were (a) terrified, (b) sick, (c) both the aforementioned, and (d) bored when they were neither (a) nor (b). As I recall, the women mostly muttered amongst themselves and never actually staged an open rebellion.

Mother didn't swim. She wore a life jacket at all times, except when we went through a lock, and then she wore three. She told us horrible stories of what would likely happen to us in the raging whirlpools inside the locks, so that we, too, would wear three.

Father raved on about the crystal pure air in the wilds of Ontario, while we gagged on the fumes from the outboard. He trolled a hookless line through the whole Trent River canal system, caught not one fish (didn't intend to), and enthused daily that yessiree, he'd fished all these waters.

We pulled into some little port, Gamebridge, I think it was, and mother bought a huge eleven-quart basket of black cherries (if she had to take part in this pleasure cruise she was damn well going to have some good food that didn't have to be cooked on a ridiculous one-burner stove — if you could call the thing a stove.) The three women ate all the cherries that same day — to relieve the boredom — and spent the next day with the runs, sprinting in to the bucket which had all the privacy of a backyard swing. Undaunted, father extolled the unparalleled beauty of the waterways unwinding before us, and burst into several verses of a bawdy Robbie Burns poem, rolling all the r's with great gusto.

One would think that the recollection of that cruise would have given me pause when, at twice the impressionable age of fourteen I became romantically interested in a soft-spoken man with serious green eyes and a ready chuckle who used all his spare time building a boat on which he planned to sail away. But no, it didn't, and the answer must be that time had a befuddled moment and left this lady not only twice as old, but twice as impressionable as well. In any case, so taken was I with Gary and his plans for a new life that the past seemed irrelevant, and one fine day I moved my belongings into the apartment in the barn where the boat was taking form, knowing full well that life with this man meant life with that boat.

And a good thing it was, too.

*   *   *

"Aren't you scared?" someone asked me before we struck out west to San Diego for our first experience at sea — a 4,000-mile offshore trip down the Pacific, through the Panama Canal and up the Caribbean on the 42' trimaran La Paz. I'd been carefully avoiding this issue, but finally had to admit that a wee corner of my mind was definitely scared. Well, actually it was a pretty big corner. This long passage in a small boat was the sort of trip from which people sometimes don't come back.

I forced myself to face the ultimate question. Would the secrets revealed be worth jeopardizing both our lives? The mere asking of that question had a wonderful effect. It gave me a chance to answer, and I heard all parts of me shout "Yes!" Hearing the answer erased all ambivalence. Apprehension faded. Excitement mounted, and developed into a state of heightened awareness and openness that stayed with me for the duration of the trip and a long time after.

Why some people say "yes" to that question and others just as vehemently say "nay" is not easily explained. Some people have a good thing going on land, so why upset the apple cart? Others feel morally bound to stay with a job or family. Still others feel that sailing is hedonistic and therefore not worthy of serious pursuit. But Gary and I could see people around us who were caught in webs. No spider was about to pounce, but neither could they change course from the sticky horizontal strands to the vertical free-flowing ones. We vowed to avoid the web. We also wanted to take positive steps to remain alive emotionally and mentally and this exciting lifestyle was, for us, the answer.

One could say that we went to sea because we were scared — scared of the consequences of not going. But that was only part of it. We also just plain liked the idea.

* * *

We have always been glad that fortune supplied us with a conservative sailor as teacher. Don McGregor, skipper of *La Paz*, was as careful a teacher as he was sailor. None of this "by guess and by golly" stuff. As he says, he's like an old grandmother with his boat. It is an approach that works, for after ten years there have been no accidents (other than falling into the engine bilge one day while watching a young woman walk past), and the boat is like new (except for the brass fittings which are pretty green because he refuses to polish away all that precious metal for which he paid good money).

Don taught us to be prudent by always, *always* thinking of the safety of the vessel first. For example, we never, no matter how tired, entered a strange port at night. On the last morning — or what we thought was going to be the last morning — of a twelve-day offshore passage, we could see Acapulco in the distance. The wind eased up and we ghosted closer, dreaming of all the delights we would find on shore that night: cold beer! ice cream! people! trees! We could hardly wait. The wind died. By sundown, we were a maddening half hour from the harbor entrance, and we knew we were doomed. A maze of harbor lights pierced the blackness and the wind began to howl. We couldn't believe it. All night we kept up a mad pace back and forth across the harbor entrance, putting mile after mile under the hulls. "Really making time!" we laughed hysterically as we roared through the water at ten knots under reefed main. Gary threw together a tuna salad using some tuna that Don had canned some time ago. We'd been already tasting shore food and we picked at it unenthusiastically.

We were exhausted by dawn, and as the sky lightened, were horrified to realize that we had gotten a good five miles of offing in our desire to be well away from uncharted hazards near shore. The wind died abruptly and it took us all day to sail in. We joked nervously about spending another night charging back and forth, as by late afternoon we were still a mile off. But a puff of breeze came out of nowhere and we dropped anchor just seconds before the sun dropped out of sight.

Maddening! But safe.

"Now that's where an engine would have come in handy," some people might say. Well, yes, I suppose so. But in our case, not even when the wind began to howl did we wish the engine was functioning or would we have accepted a tow. To all of us it was a great thrill to be operating completely under sail power. We were proud of *La Paz*, and proud of each other. And it was with tremendous satisfaction that we finally dropped the hook, thus marking the end to a 1,000-mile passage under sail alone.

* * *

At thirteen, Lew, Don's son, had his life figured out. He was finishing eighth grade by correspondence, and saw no further need for formal education for the kind of life he intended to lead. He would be on the water around boats. He did go on to take ninth grade by correspondence, in case he should change his mind. But by fourteen, he knew that formal schooling would hamper his getting the training he needed for the kind of life he wanted.

Lew plunged into experiences that would teach him more about the sea, about boat building, and about the handling of a small boat at sea. He helped to build several yachts, he crewed across the Atlantic a few times, and at fifteen he was hired as skipper of a charter boat in the Virgin Islands, a job he held for two years. He delivered boats to the United States, to Canada, and to the Islands. Now, at twenty-three, he is competent at, and can make his living from, a variety of boat-associated activities.

Lew was given responsibility early. He was making

decisions on the boat by the time he was ten. I feel that if children are given reasonable responsibility, they will learn how to handle it and have little time left for getting into trouble. Lew is a prime example of how well this theory can work out. In any case, he has been the launching point for many a heated discussion.

Some people say Lew was different, Lew was exceptional. I say he wasn't (although of course he was).

* * *

One moonless night when it was particularly rough and the direction of the seas unpredictable, we decided to heave to, hopefully bow to the seas. I took the helm, and Gary, Don and Lew tried a series of wraps, tires, para-anchors and various sail combinations to hold the head into the wind. Much straining and cursing. Nothing was successful. We then decided to let the ship lie ahull with storm staysail and trysail, the helm lashed hard over and thus making a knot or two windward. The deck heaved violently and the men inched forward in forty knots of wind to tackle the sails. A sheet whipped out of Lew's hand and snarled itself around some unknown thing high on the pitching mast. He crawled up to retrieve it.

Engrossed in their efforts, they did not see what I was looking into with disbelief — a huge sea, perhaps a good fifteen feet higher than the others (which were about twenty feet) moving toward us. I shouted, then waited, staring. At my scream the men looked up and, like fools, not one of them reached for a secure handhold. They just stood there, like me — but I, at least, had the tiller. The sea was almost upon us.

But then, incredibly, it was under us, then behind us. Unscathed, we watched it move on — imperturbable, like a silent prehistoric behemoth lumbering on with a tireless rolling gait. Later that night Don decided to put up more sail than he had previously thought prudent, and the boat rode well with the additional canvas.

Ever prompt and efficient in his role of self-critic, he winced and said, "My only regret is that I didn't put it up sooner."

Lew turned, his hands busy with reef lines, and responded with steady eyes and a deliberate, almost admonishing, voice, "Dad, never regret that you are a conservative sailor."

Don met his gaze for a moment and turned his attention to the set of the sails.   * * *

Steve and Sherri Glass sailed with us on *La Paz* for a week or so. They were building a Cross 38' and, like us, needed sailing experience. (*La Paz* was a Cross 42', and *Isla* was a Cross 46'. Quite a gathering of Cross builders, although it hadn't been planned that way.) Sherri had been vacillating for some months about making the trip. Twenty-eight, almost totally blind for several years, she had been hoping to have an operation before the trip that would return her sight at least partially. The operation had taken place, but the desired effect had not. Disappointed but not defeated, she decided that if she were not going to be given the privilege of sailing with her sight, then she would sail without it. And sail she did. She took her turn at the helm, Steve resting or chatting in the cockpit with her. She kept a windward course by listening for the slightest flutter from a sail that would head up into the wind a bit too far, then fall off, and head up into the wind again to the flutter.

They say about seasickness that you feel so miserable you're afraid you'll die, but then you get sicker and feel so much more miserable that you're afraid you won't die. And it's quite true. Sherri suffered from seasickness more than the average person, because she could not see the horizon, which is what helps many sailors retain their sense of equilibrium and the contents of their stomach. To her it was a part of boating, which she loved, so "do it and get it over with" was her philosophy. She would just quietly move to the stern and lean over, and if you didn't happen to be looking at the time, you'd never know. When *I'm* seasick, I make sure everyone knows how wretched I'm feeling.

One afternoon, in the aft cabin, Sherri and I were lying prone in a position that considerably helped our queasy stomachs. We began talking about her eyes, and she said she was taking this opportunity of sightlessness to develop her mind. She might never have gotten around to this with good eyes, because she considers sight to be somewhat thoughtless. I told her that she'd be one hell of a lady to contend with when she got her sight back, with both a mind *and* eyes. She laughed, delighted with this awesome image of herself.

One morning when we were anchored off the coast of Mexico, there was a low surf running, and Steve got out the boards. Sherri also lowered herself into the water onto a board and had Steve point her in the direction of the rollers. She didn't catch one that day, although she has at other times. Later she donned flippers and snorkle and swam around the boat, her long blonde hair spreading about her in all directions. She came back talking excitedly about some light and dark patches she'd been able to see on the bottom.

We heard talk of a little village nearby by the name of Yelapa. Although it is not far south of Puerto Vallarta, no roads lead to it, but it is accessible by a three-day mule trip, and by water. Our curiosity was piqued, so the next day we raised the drifter into a faint trace of a breeze and ghosted into the bay at Yelapa. It was a wildly beautiful place. Mountains rose precipitously out of the sea and soared hundreds of feet into the endless azure skies. Thatched-roof structures clung to cliffs. Plots of land climbing the slopes were being cultivated. White tropical birds swooped and soared against a backdrop of lush, tangled greenery. A fresh-water stream rushed into the ocean, and a pure white strip of sand separated the sea from an inviting turquoise lagoon.

We sailed closer to shore as Gary kept sounding for the bottom with the hundred-foot lead line — it appeared there was no bottom in this bay! Finally, not much more than a hundred feet from shore, the lead touched and Steve threw over the forty-five pound plow, as well as fifty feet of chain and as much of the nylon rope as he dared. It was an onshore wind and La Paz' stern was practically sitting on shore. The slope of the beach was about forty-five degrees and in spite of the light wind, an impressive swell was rolling in. La Paz, too, was rolling, and Sherri and I got that all-too-familiar feeling in our stomachs again.

The anchor seemed to be holding fine, so we all piled into the dinghy and headed shoreward to explore. Our surfing experts calculated the surf and we roared in on the top of a good one. We hit the beach like wet rags and came up laughing and spitting salt and sand. The few locals looked on, tolerantly amused. We traced the streams inland, marveled over the lushness, frolicked in the lagoon and raced up and down the sandy spit. We managed a fairly dignified departure in the dinghy, and gained some respect from the locals, or so we imagined.

The next day the swells coming in from the ocean had grown to an alarming size. Don was getting more and more agitated, and we all looked at the rocky shore in a different light. It was decided that we had better make tracks while we could.

With a boat on either side of us and the shore behind us, there was very little maneuvering room. The engine would be no help to us as it was still in the packing crate. Gary and Steve were stationed at the bow. Up with the sails. We eased off on the anchor and fell off to the port tack, hoping to brack the anchor loose as we fell off, but it held tight. Back to the starboard tack to make another pass at the anchor, then another. Tack again, and again. That anchor must have been hooked onto China. Gary and Steve could not endure the strain of hauling on the anchor much longer. Finally it popped loose, and Don, looking a couple of years older, steered the boat for open water. Gary collapsed on the deck and gasped, "We'd better sell . . . our boat . . . and buy . . . a home in the suburbs."

Puerto Vallarta was the next stop. The lights of the town were spotted during the night, which meant we had to tack back and forth across the harbor entrance until the first light of dawn could guide us safely in. Puerto Vallarta is a jet-set tourist trap, but a beautiful old town nevertheless. Official-dom was out in full force and many hours were spent between customs, immigration and the port captain's office — all of them at opposite ends of the town. They were secretly at war with each other, and not so secretly with yachtsmen. We eventually weakened and paid the graft — ten dollars. Only then did things get easier.

This was Steve and Sherri's last night on board. Tomorrow they would don backpacks and strike out homeward. Gary prepared a special treat, a double batch of fudge. We watched hypnotically as he stirred and beat until he felt that just the right moment had arrived for pouring. He waited a touch too long, and Sherri convulsed with laughter at Gary's frantic efforts and our urgent shrieks to get the stuff out before it became a permanent part of the post. We lay back, passed the dish around and let chunks of the delicious stuff melt in our mouths.

Presently, we moved into the cockpit and the relative coolness of the night air. Gary packed his pipe and picked out a gentle calypso tune on the guitar. Sherri rolled a cigarette — this kept her in touch with reality, she said.

The full moon was brilliant orange, rising above the tree-tops. When Steve directed Sherri's gaze to the spot in the sky where the moon hung, she was able to make out a faint spot of brightness. She contemplated this for a long time — as indeed, we all did.

*   *   *

My watch. No wind. All the others asleep. A freighter appeared on the horizon at 2230 hours. From the lights I could see it was on a collision course with us. No worry, it was 8 miles away. Make a log entry. Five minutes later it was considerably closer. The range lights were still in line, and both red and green running lights were visible. Too far away to worry, I decided. I looked at the drifter hanging limp on the forestay. The freighter was closer. "Surely their radar has picked us up," I thought, mildly apprehensive. To be on the safe side, I flipped on our running lights, usually left off to save the battery. About a minute later I could see only the red light, which I decided meant that the freighter had veered off to pass us to port. Or had the green light picked that moment to burn out, or had someone stepped in front of it?

The freighter was still rushing toward us at a ferocious rate. Again, to be on the safe side, I unfastened the xenon flasher from its place on the life ring and held it high. The brilliant strobe burst its staccato message into the night, lighting up our whole ship every other second, but I knew it would do us good only if someone were looking. We had read that some freighters are too short-staffed to carry full-time watches. It was really close now. I looked up at the empty heavens hoping for a sudden squall that would send some power into the helpless sail. Although I was reasonably sure it was giving us right of way, I called Don out of a deep sleep. Then I heard the engines — the ship was upon us. If Don was perturbed at the sight and sound of this freighter bearing down on us he hid it well. He took the flasher from me and stood with it on the cabin top to give it as much height as possible. The engines got louder, and thirty seconds later the freighter passed us fifty yards off the stern. The crew shone a spotlight on us, we heard them laugh, and they roared off into the blackness. I pushed my heart back down my throat and told Don to go back to sleep, thank you very much.

*   *   *

To get us both out of the noonday sun, a woman with eight children invited me into her house in a village in Costa Rica: cement floor, palm-frond walls, chickens all over the place, and the only cat in the village. She asked how many children I had, and I replied that I didn't have any and that I didn't want any. She laughed and laughed and held her sides and laughed some more.

Foreign women say unthinkable things which make them definitely funny.

* * *

Our ship was flying over the muddy, debris-laden waters of the Mohawk River. The five of us had to keep a sharp lookout for partly-submerged deadheads and even whole trees, either one of which could damage our three-quarter-inch plywood hulls.

Two inches of rain had fallen on the surrounding hills in the past twenty-four hours. All of the run-off feeds into the Mohawk River, and we could see that the river was maybe a foot above its usual level. The current had increased to four knots, leaving a deep gurgling wake as it tore past the buoys. We remembered fighting this same river under a late-May flood condition earlier that year while on our way to Canada. Several times we exclaimed how lucky we were to be going *with* the current, making such good time.

By early afternoon, we were being carried toward Lock 12 at the unprecedented speed of eight knots — the usual speed under power being four. As we rounded a bend in the river, the lock leapt into view, gates closed, a barge inside. A sightseeing boat, the *Emita II,* had turned away from it and was motoring towards us. The skipper shouted over to us, "You can't tie up at that lock — it's four inches under water!"

We had no choice but to turn back into the current and fight our way upstream to a good dock, and wait it out. An interminable two hours later we gloomily tied up at Fultonville — the trip *downstream* to the lock had taken only fifteen minutes!

By sundown the river had risen another six inches, leaving just three inches before *this* dock would be awash. The flood had not yet crested — it would rise higher. As *Isla* rose with the water, would her starboard ama float onto the dock and be left there when the flood receded? As a precaution, we contrived a wondrous system of fenders, tires and boards, and began a series of half-hour watches.

Heavy, seething masses of black clouds whipped by. The wind was gusting to fifty miles per hour and the temperature dropped into the low forties. Properly dressed, clutching a hot coffee, and warmed by thoughts of the hot buttered rum and shortbread that would emerge from the galley when the stint was over, we undertook our watches with a great deal of good cheer.

Shortly after sundown the dock was an inch under water.

She held until midnight, and then was a full two feet lower in the morning. God be praised, we'd saved the ship and all aboard!

With only the Troy lock left to descend, we rose early to get it over with and maybe get the masts up to do some sailing in the afternoon. But we were greeted with a pea-soup fog. When it appeared to be lifting, we let go the lines, but the clearing of the fog was merely a ruse, and the dank droplets enshrouded us once again. We hugged the east shore to avoid being swept over the flooded dam on the west side.

Sitting there, waiting for the Troy dock lock master to let us down this last level, we were treated to a remarkable display which surely few people have witnessed: seagulls at play. Beside us was the huge Troy dam, water flowing smoothly over the top and cascading in wild confusion onto the rocks below, sending up clouds of mist. Twenty or so gulls were sitting on the smooth racing water, stern to the dam. Each bird was carried by the current to the very edge of the dam, then just as it appeared that the bird would be swept irretrievably into the cauldron below, it would spread wide its wings and dart up and away to the front of the line to be carried once again to the precipice — obviously in the pursuit of pleasure. We watched, entranced.

When we were finally released from the Troy lock, the tension evaporated and left us all feeling quite heady. We had escaped the clutches of a raging river.

*   *   *

Warren is a tall, black-bearded Australian who fancies himself to be something of a devil-may-care adventurer. I must admit that the rougher it gets, the more he likes it — he maintains that there's nothing better than to have to change a headsail in the pouring rain, the bow heaving in a sloppy sea, the wind slicing through clothes and flesh. While the rest of us are cursing or pretending not to panic, Warren's laughter roars out across the water as if in robust thanks to the god of rough weather. He looks for all the worlds like a swashbuckling searover of years gone by.

It was his birthday, and in spite of the weather I tackled a cake in the frying pan on top of the stove. Lifting the lid a couple of times, I giggled as the batter went schloop, schloop, from side to side in the pan. Some cake! Amazingly, it did rise, and set at an intriguing angle of about twenty degrees. Warren's rough weather god must have smiled upon it.

*   *   *

What a day! We were sixty-five miles north of New York in the morning, and knew that we could make it to the city by sundown only if the right winds came up. And they did!

This part of the Hudson River is particularly breathtaking, with sheer rock rising on both sides, crowned with maples and sumac ablaze in their fall brilliance. The river itself is over half a mile wide. We surged through the water for a while at an exhilarating fourteen knots. *Isla* was performing magnificently, and it seemed to us that she knew it. We beamed as she beam reached.

Later in the afternoon, the winds became variable, changing from five to an incredible fifty knots, and shifting through ninety degrees in just minutes. R-rip! The genny blew a seam. Change headsails! Feed the main! Fend off the dinghy! Up with the drifter! Down with the drifter! Ready the anchor! In all, a tiring experience. But *good!*

We docked at the South Street Seaport Museum in a four-knot current, smack downwind of the fish plant. A rather inglorious end, we thought, sniffing, to an absolutely stupendous day.

*   *   *

I love river sailing. It gives me the feeling that I am privileged to be looking on wild and private domains. I sit there hardly breathing, all senses alert, waiting to catch glimpses of the secrets of the world.

There is no need to set up watches when we're cruising a river, because I will greedily take them all — so as not to miss a thing. And so it was that peaceful afternoon on the secluded Pungo River. I sat on the wheel house, reaching my legs through the hatch to grasp the wheel with my toes, and looking all about me as the boat whispered through the still water at one or two knots. The tips of the sails caught little bits of wind over the treetops.

We have a tradition on our boat that whoever is on watch gets waited upon. This is to keep the watchperson from dashing into the galley for snacks and leaving the helm untended, and as a kind of compensation for sticking out the watch period which can be boring — especially if everyone is down below, out of earshot. I am not sure just how much the opportunity of being waited upon affected my offer to take all the watches that day, but I do remember joyously calling down quite frequently for goodies from the galley. Somebody made pan after pan of mock pizza, using stale bread for the pastry, and I recall demolishing quite a number of them.

What a fine day!

Shortly after sundown, we slid quietly aground.

"Hey, we've stopped!"

"You were too close to that bank!"

"We've been that close all along!"

"Get the engine going — we have to reach town before it's totally black!"

"The engine's overheating!"

"Quick, get some water, pour it in!"

"The water's not doing any good!"

"Yes it is!"

"No it isn't!"

"Better kedge off, get the Danforth!"

"Here, row it out!"

"It's dragging!"

"!%â)(*!!"

"Give me the Plow!"

"No, not that side, the other side!"

"Don't forget you have to lead it outside these shrouds!"

"!%&#*!"

"I can't see you, where are you?"

"Winch it in!"

"I'll get in the water and push the bow at the same time!"

"%&$*! It's cold!"

"Get the engine going again!"

"%&â*!. It's hot!"

"Push!"

"Pull!"

"We're off!"

Great cheers.

Ah. The quiet peace of river sailing.

* * *

Harry was a man of average height and weight, of "a certain age," and would in fact have been absolutely average if he did not get at times quite a mad, knowing look in his eyes. He was from somewhere in Canada, and people ("they," he called them) from everywhere else were "after him."

A norther hit just as we were rounding Frying Pan Shoals. Although the wind was with us, we were careening up and over fifteen-foot waves that were created by the southerly set of the Gulf Stream flowing into the strong northerly winds. Later, with the wind veering to the port quarter, the seas increased to twenty feet. Warren and I retreated to our prone positions. Pokey, our resident canine, would not risk the foredeck and converted her spot under the table to her own private bathroom. One meal of chili and another of mulligan stew flew to the floor. The helmsman was constantly soaked. Several gallons of Atlantic ocean poured through a hatch, which had been inadvertently left undogged.

The running lights were getting dim, and Gary started the engine to recharge the batteries. It was dead. Thinking he'd found the cause, he drilled a hole in the muffler to drain it of the water it had taken on in those high seas. The engine still would not start. Salt water in the engine? That could be serious.

No doubt about it, this was a rough passage.

Harry was at the helm, and Gary was beside him checking the seas, the engine and the shortened sail. Harry fixed him with a knowing eye and said, "Gary, it's okay, I'm ready to die."

"Don't worry, Harry, I'm not."

Harry was adamant. "But Gary, really, I am ready, so it's okay."

Eventually the seas abated, and we sailed into St. Augustine. A mile offshore the wind died completely, and we'd never have made it into port except that the tide was running with us. The calm of the harbor was heaven, and we all laid back. Harry's eyes were gleaming, however, and we suspected he would rather still be facing the fury of the Atlantic.

Harry left the boat soon after that, saying that he had to return to Canada. We have never heard from or of him, and sometimes wonder, in all seriousness, if "they" got him.

* * *

It would be difficult to imagine anything more idyllic.

I lay face down on the gently sloping seashore of a tiny island, toes dug into the moist coolness closer to the water's edge, fingers stretched out across unbelievably white sand

and just barely touching the relaxed fingers of my skipper. A blazing sun beat down on our bronzed skin. Just as we would get uncomfortably hot, and think that we couldn't take it any longer, the surf would roll up over our bodies and cool us off delightfully. As it retreated, the water seeping back to the sea made little, pleasant popping sounds — minute bubbles that burst all around us, releasing the slightly pungent, almost musty odor of a clean seashore that seems to smell of life itself.

We could hear the surf crashing a hundred feet to the north of us where ragged limestone outcroppings encroached upon the beach. Opening one eye, I watched it froth up into mounds of foam, hesitate a moment, then tumble back among the rocks.

My eye roved inland and rested on a small pine tree, fated at some prior time to point perpetually westward because of the trade winds that swept constantly over the island from the east. Its claim to fame was two-fold: it marked the highest point on the island, eight feet above sea level; and it was the only tree on the island. Sweeping further, my eye contemplated a conical white light tower, not much taller than the pine tree. And beyond that, at the very tip of the island, a grey heron, head cocked to one side, listened for sounds of life in the sand.

An unparalleled vacation. Everything the posters had promised: the serenity, the untouched beaches, limitless sun and sea, timeless moments for lovers of all ages...

This island and all its delights were the things we used to dream about during the six years it took to build *Isla*. But now the boat was a wreck, and gone. Gone, too, was the well-stocked galley, and our supply of drinking water was running low...

Had we paid too dearly to be here? We dared not to talk about it.

*   *   *

According to plan, *Isla* was on the homeward leg of a two-month Caribbean cruise. A sense of well-being pervaded the whole boat and its crew. Even Pokey seemed to be, more than usual, at one with the universe, as she gazed through slitted eyes at the serenity of the sea.

Behind us were a myriad of adventures in the Spanish-speakng Dominican Republic and French-speaking Haiti. We had plunged into these two languages and cultures, acquiring friends, haggling vociferously in the market, buying mementoes, teaching English to the "jamais dodos" (the ladies of the night or, literally, the "never sleeps") who were working to make money to buy their passage out of Haiti, and riding tired donkeys up treacherous mountain paths to the monstrous fortress of his majesty, King Henri Christophe.

Ahead of us now stretched two weeks of diving, snorkling, shelling on deserted beaches, and hours of lying on deck as we sailed leisurely through the island-studded, turquoise waters of the Bahamas. *Isla* was coming into her own. The dreams of the six building years were emerging into reality. Immersed in private worlds, we contemplated the days past and the delights to come...

I had the six to eight o'clock watch, and printed in the log, "LOVE IT!" The night was absolutely clear, there was a bright moon on the wane, there were millions of stars that we could pick out like old friends ("Look, there's Betelgeuse, and Sirius, and..."), and the sea was slightly ruffled from the freshened wind blowing steadily on the beam at six to ten knots.

Gary took the eight to ten watch, and wrote, "Beautiful Sailing!"

Harry took the ten to twelve watch. He never finished it. I was jolted out a deep sleep at 11:30.

Coral! It sounded like coral on the hull. The crashing and crunching exploded in my brain, and a needle of ice stabbed my heart. I tore up on deck, shock reverberating through my whole body. White water was breaking all around us — beyond that, total blackness. And looking over the side I saw what I knew I would see — masses of coral heads glimmering quietly a mere foot under the surface. *Isla* drew three feet six inches. We were in trouble.

I'd had a premonition of this two weeks earlier while anchoring among coral heads that had plenty of depth, as we had many times. An image had flashed for an instant into my mind's eye of *Isla* impaled on a shallow coral reef, and, had realized at that moment that coral was *Isla*'s only real enemy. And now, here we were. I forced myself to be calm. A panic-stricken idiot would be of no use to us now.

This was no slight brush against a coral head. The ocean had lifted *Isla*'s ten tons like a toy and dropped her down onto a bed of jagged staghorn coral whose rapacious fingers were now jabbing through the thin skin of the hull. Five minutes earlier we had been in 1500 feet of ocean, and now we were trapped on this shallow reef, encircled by seething destruction.

It was high tide, someone announced after checking the tide tables. Nobody said a word. We all knew that was the worst news we could possibly have had at that moment.

We lowered the sails and fired the engine. It came to life immediately and gave us a spark of hope, but the boat did not budge.

John and Rick, on board for the past month, launched the dinghy, planning to probe the area around us for the nearest good water. But the surf was crashing so violently around us that the little boat became a crazed beast in the water, and we hauled it back on board before it capsized, or filled with water, or got damaged by smashing into *Isla*.

Our chances were diminishing.

The tide ran out. The line of breaking surf, frothing white against the black sea and sky, receded onto the reef behind us, and the motion decreased. Here and there arms of coral emerged from their watery lair, probing the night air as if in search of new prey.

An hour after we hit, the keel had gone and there was water above the floor boards in the main salon. This did not mean we were sinking — how can you sink on a shallow reef? It did not even mean that we would sink in deeper water should we float free, because the outriggers would keep the boat floating high. Even if both floats were holed, *Isla* would still float like a barge because she was made of wood and was not ballasted. My only fear as to the safety of us all was that, like a piece of wood on coarse sandpaper, *Isla* would gradually be ground down to so little that rough weather could break her up.

The light we had been looking for all evening hove clearly into view when the moon set — directly in line with it — at a bearing of 284 degrees. At least now we knew where we were: on the eastern-most edge of the reef, four miles from the nearest uninhabited land, forty miles from the nearest inhabited land.

Both Gary and I knew that had we been alone we might have taken our chances with *Isla*, news of heavy weather coming and all. She was part of us. Perhaps at the next high tide something could be done to free the hulls from the coral. She could be towed back to Miami. But there were four others involved here who had not counted on shipwreck. Nor had we, of course, but we'd always known it could happen.

We set out for tiny North West Cay in the morning, in the ship's two dinghies.

Food already had a new flavor — the spice of diminishing supply — and we chewed carefully the few raisins that I doled out.

Everyone except Gary kept up a steady banter during the four-hour row to the island.

"Harry's the fattest, so we'll eat him first," decided John.

"I must warn you," defended Harry, "I'm on antibiotics. Besides, I'm old — I'll be tough and stringy."

Laughter.

"Hey, Dee," Rick called out from the *Zodiac*, "seeing as you're the only woman on the island, I'd like to propose."

"Well, let's see," I considered. "What are you offering as a dowry?"

"Oh, a few wet cigarettes ..."

More laughter. They all knew I hated cigarettes in any shape or form.

Gary's hands were beginning to blister, and I wrapped several layers of gaffer's tape around them. Bleeding hands would impede survival on the island and return trips to *Isla*.

"Hey, what do we do if a shark comes bumping along this rubber raft?" hollered Mike.

"Don't worry," I reassured him as I looked nervously about for dorsal fins, "sharks like deeper water." And in an aside to Gary, "I hope."

We were all ashore, and for the first time in twelve hours we smiled real smiles. Pokey claimed the island with a long pee, grinned at us and trotted off to explore.

On the east beach, there was a huge pile of some three to four hundred conch shells. They still retained much of their vibrant living color, and they were still reeking from unremoved gus. Obviously, someone had been here recently, conching. Would they be back for more? Beside the pile of shells was a not-too-old empty packet of Dominican cigarettes. Had our concher come all the way from the Dominican Republic? Was he a poacher? A poacher, we realized, would perhaps shy away if he saw people.

Upon checking the Bahamas Yachtmen's Guide, we read that, "Over the centuries, Hogsty Reef has proven a graveyard for shipping." In our daily dives for food we were able to verify this. Gary found wedged among coral heads the teak cabin side of a wooden yacht fastened with brass and copper nails. Mike uncovered a hundred-pound kedge anchor, flaking with rust. Here and there were pieces of a steel ship, a bank of ship's batteries, and other items too coral-encrusted to identify. We hoped the crews of these vessels had fared as well as we had.

One day, Mike and I spent the afternoon writing up S.O.S. messages (the apparent futility of which amused the others) and putting them into clear glass bottles that we found washed up on the island. We tied strips of glo-orange cloth around the necks to make them more visible. Mike threw them as far out to sea as he could on the west side of the island. "Probably end up in Cuba where they won't understand them anyway," we thought. As it turned out, one of these bottles *was* picked up about three weeks later — by an Ohio student on vacation on Long Island in the Bahamas, some 200 miles north-west of us. Most of the message had been obliterated, but my parents' telephone number was still intact. He called them, and he was surprised to learn the message came from a real shipwreck. Months later he wrote that he had mounted the message on a bronze plaque and hung it in his recreation room. If help had not found us on the twelfth day, that bottle might have been our salvation.

We all knew that a ship sighted did not mean rescue. Nevertheless, there was great excitement the first day that we spotted a ship on the horizon. We raced into preplanned action. Mike got a smoky fire going. Gary began signaling with the mirror. John and I stood on the island's highest point and waved a red blanket. Mike climbed the tower and waved the glo-orange tarp. All to no avail. Eventually these rescue operations became almost irrelevant to our survival. They were an intrusion (fourteen of them in all) on the daily routine.

The night watch routine involved walking to the tower every fifteen minutes to make a careful sweep of the horizon for ships. One night during Gary's watch, I could not sleep, and the two of us walked together to the tower. We held each other close for a long time, each thinking about *Isla*, and the precariousness of our present position. Groping for some-thing positive to say, I finally said, in a voice that seemed strange to me, "I know everything will be alright in the long run, but it sure is a shame."

"It sure is," he said, and held me tighter.

And then, leaving almost everything unsaid, we picked our way back to the shelter, accompanied every four seconds by the flash of the beacon as it blinked its mindless message into the empty blackness of the night.

One day I caught John engaging in a strange ritual wherein he massaged yet more oil into his bronzing body, and alternately sucked in his stomach and flexed his biceps.

"What *are* you doing?" I teased.

He paused for a moment, and then replied in his most reasonable voice, "I want to look my best for the cameras when they come to rescue us." Suck, flex, suck ...

At sundown on the 12th day, Gary was just returning from the water's edge. He had been cleaning the conch that would be Pokey's supper, a conch that Rick (still weak from dysentry) had dived for earlier that day. As he approached the shelter, Rick suddenly pointed out to sea in the direction from which Gary had just come.

"It's a boat," he said quietly. "It's a goddamn boat."

Sure enough, a thirty-foot power boat was nosing into the beach. We hadn't seen it until it was 200 yards away because it had come right out of the setting sun. We hadn't heard it because it was downwind.

Everyone started leaping and shouting. Suddenly, with horror, we realized that they were't putting down anchor — they might be leaving! The dinghy was on the west side of the island, so Gary grabbed his fins and swam out to the boat. Meanwhile, the other four guys ran the dinghy over to the west side of the island.

Gary reported later that the man and woman on board surveyed him apprehensively as he emerged at the stern of their boat. The woman was very nervous, and asked, "Wh-what do you want?" Gary explained that we'd been ship-wrecked and stranded here for twelve days, and she said with noticeable relief, "Is this for real?"

Frank and Wendy were delivering the thirty-two-foot *Trojan* to the Virgins, and pulled in here to anchor for the night and transfer some fuel. They had heard many stories of piracy, and when they saw these strange-looking people running wildly about this little hump of sand in the open

Atlantic, they had considered pulling away and leaving us. It was lucky Gary swam out when he did!

From the island we could see the *Trojan* with Gary aboard motoring around to the east beach. Thinking they planned to anchor there, the guys ran the dinghy back to that side. The captain must not have liked what he saw there because he then motorized back to the west side and dropped the hook. The dinghy then ran back across the island to the west side. I'd never seen them move that fast!

Gary wrote later in his log: From the flying bridge of the *Trojan* we kept seeing this eight-legged dinghy roar back and forth across the island. Captain Frank eyed them suspiciously — they *did* look like a boarding party, John with his flowing mane of beard and hair, Rick with a great diving knife strapped to his leg. They were a cutthroat-looking bunch! I tried to smile reassuringly.

The *Trojan* carried four of us the next day to South Caicos, 90 miles southeast. I arranged for a U.S. Coast Guard helicopter to pick up Gary, Mike and Pokey, and the salvaged gear.

Finally, after many changes of plan, we had word that the helicopter would be bringing Gary, Mike and Pokey at 5:30 that very afternoon. The time came and went, and I stewed over all the things that might have gone wrong. At 6:30, WHERE WERE THEY? And would the helicopter be a big one, big enough to accommodate all the gear, too? At 7:00, word came through that they were off course, running out of fuel, and might have to land at Great Inagua 100 miles away. Oh no! I stewed and sweated.

At 7:30, someone called out, "There they are!" I ran to the door and flew down the steps. Embracing Gary, Mike and Pokey all at the same time, I asked about the gear. "That's what she's really worried about," laughed Gary.

I chirped and burbled and chirped some more. No one really seemed to notice, and I really didn't care.

Isla was us. We were *Isla*. Perhaps too much so. Losing her was like losing ourselves.

We were flown out of South Caicos by a fellow whose name I have forgotten, but he was Lenny Bruce's lawyer.

"Your present position in life is really exciting," he enthused to us. "I'm envious."

Here's a real weirdo, I thought to myself.

"Yes," he carried on, "you have been thrown into the

fertile void. Anything at all can happen, because nothing is there."

He beamed at us with the logic of it all, and we stared back at him blankly.

As it turned out, he wasn't too far off.

*   *   *

Something about her appealed to us, but we haven't to this day put our finger on exactly what it was. Cliff, the owner of the yard in St. Petersburg where we found her, was going to burn her.

"I can understand buying a low-cost trim one that needs some work," said Cliff. "But," he continued, his voice rising with good-humored indignation, "why *that* one?"

"We have practically no money," explained Gary, laughing, "but we do have the building skills. So, she's the perfect boat for us. Right?"

"Right," responded Cliff, always willing to back a dreamer.

The boat in question was a Cross 28' — a round-bilge trimaran sloop. Rot ran rampant. Tiny green plants grew out of the rich, composting stringers. I joked about having salad greens at our fingertips, but neither of us laughed. Our probing fingers had pushed right through the main hull. The cabin sides gaped gray and ragged. Glass was lifting in sheets off the decks. The very bow of the main hull had been patched with a big blob of black goop. The whole boat, inside and out, was soaking wet.

Feeling a trifle silly at even considering such a total wreck, we had gone below and sat down on the settee, which almost crumpled under our weight. Could we really breathe new life into this derelict? The cross beams were in excellent shape, as were keel and keelson. We sneaked looks at each other, each wondering what the other was thinking. Gary caught my eye, and we found ourselves nodding, almost imperceptibly. And because she was anything but pretty, we called her the prettiest name we could think of — *Mariposa*, which means butterfly in Spanish. Later we learned that the butterfly is a symbol of rebirth. It was to be her rebirth, and ours.

Somehow, under Gary's guidance *Mariposa* was transformed into a good little home and sailing craft.

At the time, my belly was growing to gigantic proportions, and I wondered how it could ever get any bigger (but of course it did). I spent several days wedged in the small lazarette, finishing it off so that all the debris stored temporarily in the forecastle could be permanently stowed in the aft compartment. The forecastle could then be converted into a nursery. I spent one whole day painting the lazarette with a sparkling white two-part epoxy paint, me and the bulging belly wedged between bilge and overhead, sucking in air through a piece of plastic tubing clenched in my teeth so that the noxious vapors could harm neither me nor our unborn Ben.

"Are you going to live ashore when the baby is born?" some friends asked.

"Oh no," I answered with great naïve aplomb. "We can't see why having a baby should change our lives. Come and see how we've fixed up the foc's'le ..." They would ooh and aah, and I would quietly congratulate myself that the baby had not forced us into compromise.

However, living aboard with a baby, we later discovered with something approaching alarm, was not at all the same as cruising with just the two of us. Life on board no longer revolved around the boat, it revolved around the baby. Boats and the sea had been the focus of our lives for ten years. So intent were we upon not foresaking our lifestyle that we resisted refocussing until long after the image had clouded.

We're told that the first two years of life are the crucial ones in the formation of a person's disposition. There's no doubt in my mind that the cruising environment ranks high. The air is clean, the sunshine plentiful, the motion of the sea soothing, the pace of life gentle, the mood mellow. Usually.

One big plus to sailing with a baby is that he and his daddy have much more opportunity to interact than in the usual situation where the father is home for only a few hours every evening, and then is often too tired to want to do much with the little one. The boating father has a unique chance to experience first-hand the ups and downs of rearing his own child. Not only does this create the potential for a close bond between the father and baby/child/adult, it also creates a deeper understanding between the parents, as will any role exchange. Just as the woman, who participates fully in the handling of the boat, can better appreciate why the man takes pride in certain things, why he fumes or chuckles, so the participating father can better understand the joys and frustrations of mom's day.

Because we both knew that life afloat would be a good environment in which to raise little Ben, we set out to carry on with our lives. The succeeding sixteen months were filled with laughter, tears, elation, despair, beautiful sailing, bloody awful sailing, and the snapping of endless rolls of film of Benjamin Taylor Hodgkins.

If anyone had told me a few years back that catnip tea would be at the top of my list for stocking the galley, I'd have laughed myself silly. With Ben aboard it's a must. I will leave port without sugar, coffee, toothpaste, a new ring for the pressure cooker or clean clothes, but never without at least half a pound of catnip tea. Why? Because it helps to resolve conflict between the baby's schedule and the boat's.

Like the night we departed Florida on the tail end of a norther. We were taking the chance, as is common among boats crossing the Stream in winter, that the wind would not veer north before arrival in the Bahamas. But, two hours offshore, the wind outguessed us and veered northerly picking up to twenty knots. This resulted in ten-foot choppy seas. And because *Mariposa* was an as yet untried vessel, we beat our way back to port, dropping anchor at sunup. Ben, of course, had slept through all the sail changes and bashing into waves, and at this moment peered out from the forecastle with a ready-for-action smile on his bright little face. "Oh no you don't," I countered with a ready-for *re*-action smile on *my* bright little face and I reached for the catnip tea. Five minutes later he was sleeping again, and so were mom and dad.

Mariposa hung straight back on her anchor with the outgoing current as I sat in the cockpit nursing Ben. I could look out over the infinite variety of blues and yellows on the banks, and listen to Gary rustle up some pancakes. We ate slowly and revelled in the cool, calm breeze, the quiet beauty of the islands to either side of us, and the coziness of our little boat. We had just picked our way across the banks from Salt Pond on Long Island in the Bahamas the day before, dragging the keel much of the way, and were heading back to Georgetown. Depending on the weather, it could be a two-day trip.

I laid Ben on the starboard bunk, pulled down the fish net to convert the bunk into a playpen, and went up on deck to help ready the boat. The wind and the current were with us, so we could get underway without recourse to the engine, an operation that delights us both. Up with the main sail, up with the anchor, and we slip soundlessly away.

In the dark blue of deep water, the wind picked up to fifteen knots and *Mariposa* responded comfortably by pressing her leeward hull a little deeper into the gentle swells. Routinely, but with little hope, Gary set up the trolling line. We hadn't caught a fish in days.

The islands faded behind us, and we were alone on the sea. For us, being out of sight of land is the high point of any trip — the total independence of it, the knowledge that you are completely on your own. The expanse of the universe is apparent, and the mind expands to become a part of it. When land is in sight, you are either trying to get away from it or trying to reach it. When it has faded from sight over the stern, and is not yet in sight off the bow, the mind roams unfettered for a while.

It was a glorious day. The wind picked up a little, and by mid-afternoon we were sorting our way through Hog Cay Cut, expecting to go aground any minute as it was very shallow and the tide was falling. But we had at least a foot to spare, which was a wide margin indeed after leaving furrows behind us everywhere the day before.

No sooner were we in deep water again on the other side of the cut than the trolling line went taut, and Gary hauled in the largest hogfish I have ever seen. He let the line play out again, and it was just seconds before he was hauling in a good-sized gray snapper. And then another one.

We were sure the wind would suddenly die, forcing us to anchor before reaching port, but no, it was steady and just a bit forward of the beam. It was the kind of almost surrealistic sailing that occurs when you are close to land with a good offshore breeze. Hardly a ripple on the water, and *Mariposa*'s hulls cleaved the water like three dolphins in a perfect performance.

As we approached Georgetown harbor, the wind did abate. We considered using the engine, but preferred instead to have a perfect ending to a perfect day — we ran the drifter up the forestay and ghosted quietly in through the savory supper smells emerging from a dozen of boats sitting snuggly at anchor. We dropped the sails, dropped the hook, and set about making culinary scents of our own.

A heavy dew was already falling now that the sun was gone, and Gary set up our yellow and white striped boom tent, hanging the lantern under it at the end of the boom. We took the pan-broiled snapper into the cockpit and enjoyed it in silence, looking about us at the stars and the always reassuring lights of the other boats.

Gary caught my eye and chuckled for no other reason than that everything was fine.

"Mm-m," I said in total agreement.

"Da-ooh-ah-bee-mm!" agreed Ben with a shriek.

PART II
Galleys Are Not Kitchens
"Galley" vs. "Kitchen"

I resent the recent trend in advertising to refer to galleys as kitchens. We all know that is a sales gimmick aimed at the buyer's woman. The advertiser assumes that the buyer will be male, and that his mate will need to be placated to approve the outrageous toy her husband wants to buy. Hence the word "kitchen." It is meant to soothe her, to reassure her that the boat really is quite a normal thing after all, and while she would have difficulty in seeing herself in a "galley," she will most certainly feel immediately at home in a kitchen. The use of the word belittles a woman's ability to adapt, to imagine, to yearn after adventure, to grasp new concepts, to be open to different ideas, to discern belittlement and to learn a new word.

In addition, this crass word is an insult to the centuries of seafaring tradition. It does not appear in nautical dictionaries, nor do sailors use it when referring to the cook's domain. Calling the galley a kitchen is like calling the skipper the head of the house, or the aft cabin a back bedroom. The oily use of the word is an affront to the memory of days when there were more important things than selling and conning. And it is an affront to the people who spent the majority of their lives on board ship, in a specialized life that demanded preciseness of word for survival.

Chapter 1:
Keep a Good Cook

The first law of the sea: *Keep a good watch.* I've never heard of a law that came second, but it might well be: *Keep a good cook.*

Whether the ship's cook is a permanent mate or a hired hand, the cook performs a basic ship duty, three times a day, foul weather or fair, at sea or in port. On most boats it is the role that demands the heaviest workload. Because people must eat, there is no rest for the cook.

Add to this situation the fact that the cook is excluded from the ship life or from company's conversation while a meal is being prepared, and you have all the ingredients for a mutiny. Or the cook may decide to forgo the formalities of a mutiny and jump ship. Neither is uncommon. And as one woman pointed out to me, having other boaters over for dinner is their major form of entertainment, and it doesn't seem right to her that she should have to miss half the entertainment by being down below getting dinner. Many things have boiled over in their galley, she says, and not just on top of the stove.

There's no doubt that, on some boats at least, the cook feeling left out is a real problem. What do you do about it?

First of all, there's the location of the galley. It should be between the cockpit and the main salon so that the cook is not excluded from conversation by the physical layout of the boat. This location also makes it easy for anyone who may want to offer assistance. And it facilitates serving meals, as both dining spots are only an arm's length away. Some boats have the galley forward of the main dining area, and this would be very frustrating when guests are gathered in the cockpit, as they often are. It would also be annoying, and dangerous in some conditions, to have to cart dinner those extra careening feet to the helmsman on watch.

Second, open bulkheads between the galley and main salon will facilitate verbal and visual communication. Many sailors who have had years of experience cooking on board point this out as a major feature in the galley of their choice. Margaret Roth, of the *Whisper*, is one.

Third, one or more (depending on the size of the boat) ports that open to the cockpit will, again, facilitate verbal and visual communication. If large enough, this port can be a fast way of passing out a plate of goodies or a drink. And it adds extra ventilation to an area that often gets uncomfortably steamy. One more point in its favor, this port allows the cook to see what's going on in the outside world when the companionway is closed to keep out the weather.

And fourth, side ports that open or not should also be considered, so that the cook might catch a glimpse of the flock of geese, the wake tearing past the buoy or the skinny-dipping off the Chinese junk. Anything to avoid that hemmed-in, cut-off feeling.

If you're looking for a new boat, keep an eye open for the above four features, with the well-being of your cook in mind — it may be you. If you have a permanent love affair with your current boat, consider adding some of those features.

This knotty problem can also be attacked from other angles!

For instance, why not take turns at galley duty? I know there are many skippers who snort at this idea, but the truth of the matter is that a skipper who cannot or will not function in his own galley is not worth the teak he's standing on (which, I admit, may be considerable these days). Gary and I once sailed with two other people for three months in the Pacific, and we rotated cook duty by the day. That worked well. It was heaven for me, as the only woman aboard, to not have my shipboard role prepegged by sex. And it was during those three months that I became a sailor, that I learned to sail and to love it. There's no doubt that I'd not have been much of a sailor at the end of those three months if the majority of my time had been spent in the galley.

For the men on board, this rotating of cook duty was also a liberating experience. They delved into the mysteries of haute cuisine, and found that they enjoyed it. They took pride in adding a new skill to their ability to be self-sufficient. And although this may sound like an exaggeration, it is not: galley duty on board that ship became an adventure.

An alternative to rotating cook duty would be to give the cook two or three days off per week (even one would be a welcome revolutionary change on some boats). Or, duties can be traded for one or two or three days. This would mean that if there are two people aboard, the skipper makes meals while the cook whips lines or scrubs barnacles. The idea is that, if not stuck all the time in the galley, the cook will have far greater opportunity to take part in the conversation and life of the ship. Not only will the cook stay happier this way, but when the time off is used for shipboard activities, the cook becomes a more willing and effective deck hand. And it's nice to know you can count on the cook in an emergency.

One woman told me that on her boat, when everyone else is relaxing or watching the sunset, she is invariably rushing to prepare drinks for cocktail hour, rushing through meal preparations, or rushing through the dishes. Her solution to this would be to have one person responsible for drinks, another for the meal, another for dishes. Unfortunately, her skipper would have none of it. Was he selfish? Or lazy? Or insecure? Maybe he was just a creep.

Quite a few boats operate under the theory that everyone should be able to relax either before or after a meal. On these boats, whoever cooks gets out of doing the dishes, and vice versa. This is very civilized, and harmony usually reigns. These are the boats where you find the woman changing head sails on a plunging foredeck, not because she was ordered to, but because such participation is part of the give-and-take relationship, and a part of life aboard. Because it is her adventure, too — she's not just tagging along.

Some men are disappointed that their woman does not take to boats. (A few actually frown on their woman's participation in extra-galley activities, but these, probably, are an endangered species, and no one seems too worried about their near extinction.) Of those who are disappointed, a percentage has forgotten, I think, that most girls are not raised, as are boys, to think of boating as a desirable occupation. Unless given the opportunity to change this outlook, it is reasonable to expect women to go on feeling this way. It is a mistake, made by both men and women, to assume the woman will be happier in the galley where things are familiar (that's a laugh!) than on deck. Only on deck can she learn the joys of sailing, and develop perchance a love for boat, water and weather. Only then will she be motivated to stand at her skipper's side through fog, headwinds and anchor watches, and want to go out again. Yes! Get her out of the galley! And the corollary: put someone else in.

I met a remarkable young woman several years ago aboard a sixty-five ton schooner, the *Nomad*, in the Panama Canal. She was the hired cook and spent ten hours a day preparing meals for the four crew members and serving tea on a silver tray between meals. Her desire to take part in ship life was so keen that she begged them to let her take over the night watch if they were not feeling up to it. They called on her almost every night, and never returned the favor by helping out in the galley the next day. The amazing thing is, she didn't mind. She was thrilled to have that chance to be a real part of the ship. She was surely one of a kind. There are other cooks who have this same desire, but how many with her determination and stamina?

Another practice that will help to keep the cook satisfied is reciprocity. That is, cater to the cook. Cook spends most of the day catering to captain and crew. Cater back. The galley is cook's domain and should be treated accordingly. If the cook wants an extractor fan, get it. If it's a knife rack, make one. If it's a port that gives her a view of the horizon, fine. If it's wallpaper that makes you dizzy, stick the stuff up and smile. And if it's a pre-dinner rum, get a whole case on board.

A word of warning. It may be a mistake to give the cook full rein if the acquaintance has not been a long one. We ran into a boat in Acapulco on which the bushy-bearded skipper was a professor of English back in the States. He had just taken on four new crew, the last four having jumped ship minutes after arriving in Acapulco for some reason unknown to us. Karen, in her early twenties, hitchhiking through Mexico and bubbling all over with the exuberance of her adventures, was one of the new crew. She told us the skipper had volunteered to stock the boat for the next leg of the trip, about a two-week offshore sail down the coast to Punta Arenas. All well and good. The heavy boat slipped ponderously out to sea soon after, and we figured it would reach Punta Arenas before we did. After two days we weighed anchor, and reached port thirteen days and two gales later. We looked around for Karen and her boat, eager to swap sea stories, but the boat was another two days arriving. It was then that we heard the tale.

The captain, they'd discovered when they were five miles out to sea, was on an all-rice diet. He had stocked the boat with hundred pounds of rice and nothing else. The crew was duly horrified, but they were already into the trip, the wind was fair, and adventure was in the air. They decided they could live for two weeks on rice, and all the fish they would be catching. Two days out, the first gale hit and the boat took on a lot of water. All the rice got wet, and it rotted. There was then nothing on board to eat. And the fish weren't biting.

The crew lay for five days (two gales one right after the other) in a miserable heap of cabin sole, wretching out their insides. Finally they caught one fish, a big dorado, and they were so hungry they ate it raw. When the gales abated they were four hundred miles offshore, and tried to motor in. But the engine was dead. Fortunately, a fishing vessel spotted them and towed them back. To hear Karen tell it, they'd had a marvellous time. She raved about what a pretty boat it was, the beauty of the sea when the weather turned fair, and her all-over tan. But they'd had enough of that cook. Since the cook and captain were one and the same, there was no hope of getting rid of him, so it was once again time for "musical boats." Karen bounced away, high on life. The point is this: cater to the cook, yes, but when he totes aboard a hundred-pound bag of rice, watch out.

Another thing: always be appreciative about the meals that come out of the galley. In the first place, from the global point of view, it is the privilege of a rather small minority to have ample food on the table three times a day, and this is reason enough to voice some appreciation. In the second place, a meal is a performance of sorts, and if no one applauds, why perform? (Not that a standing ovation is required every time.) In the third place, there are many times when it is a miracle that anything at all comes out of the galley, times when a simple meal requires superhuman effort. If you accept such a meal as if it were your God-given right, then the cook could not be blamed for dumping the hot stew in your lap — and if you happened to be nude at the time, so much the better. It's like any situation: if you're appreciated, you glow. If not, you go.

Something that should be routine ship procedure is to

instruct all those who come aboard for any length of time on how to operate the stove. In this way, between-meal snacks or coffees can be prepared by those who want them. It relieves the cook's never-stop, on-duty-round-the-clock feeling.

If all else fails, and you find you're stuck in the galley three times a day, seven days a week, or every time you go aboard for a weekend, there are a few tricks you can use. You might prepare most of a meal before company comes. Or you might plan a barbecue, so that someone else shoulders part of the load. Every time someone asks, "Can I help?" you might have small jobs thought out in advance so that you can say, "You sure can!" instead of the slightly martyrish "No thanks, this is a one-man galley" line. You might pull a "Tom Sawyer." Or you could try sprucing up the galley so that it looks like a fun place to be, thereby attracting helpers. By announcing, "We're fasting tonight," you could get some positive action — somebody might offer to treat the group to dinner ashore. However, you might also produce negative action, like getting yourself keelhauled. Everything has its risks.

It is true that shipboard cooks sometimes see themselves as members of an oppressed group and are, in fact, sometimes oppressed. I am reminded of an analogy that comes to us from black American literature about a raisin in the sun. What happens to a raisin in the sun, the poet asks. Does it "wither?" Does it "rot?" Or does it "EXPLODE?" The message is clear. Oppression breeds nothing good. Unless a long-overdue mutiny is a good thing in itself.

So a rule of thumb is: if you can keep the cook happy, you may keep the cook. And if you keep the cook, your body will be well-maintained. And a well-maintained body keeps a better watch than one that is not. What more could you ask?

Chapter 2:
Fire!

"YOU LENT THE FIRE EXTINGUISHER TO WHOM?"

A few hot coals in a box of sand — that's what is used to cook meals on native boats around the world. But fire is not a major hazard, and is in fact rare on these boats which do not carry fire extinguishers.

The first time I saw red coals glowing in a bucket of sand on a native boat, I was quite taken aback — how could these veteran sailors consider cooking so casually and carelessly? But to think about it, what could be safer than to have your cook fire sitting in the middle of the substance that could smother it if necessary? The nature of charcoal itself precludes the type of flash fire or explosion that can be disastrous to the modern, well-equipped boat.

I'm not advocating that we all run out and replace the galley stove with a box of sand. But I believe that we tend to think, indeed we *want* to think (as we take in the stove's chrome surfaces and shiny knobs) that they are foolproof. They exude efficiency and lull us into forgetfulness.

Fire in the modern boat, however, must be considered a distinct possibility. Every year, boats and lives are lost to flames or explosion. The cause of fire is not necessarily the result of carelessness — mistakes will happen. And it is simply not possible to be on guard 100 per cent of the time. But a number of preventive steps can be taken to minimize the frequency of fires, and insure that any mistakes made will be small.

No one safety feature should be relied on to safeguard your boat against something as dangerous as fire. Don't fall into the trap of thinking you're safe because you've got a fire extinguisher and stainless steel counters, and your propane tank vents outside. You have approached a fair measure of safety if you have incorporated twenty of the following safety features or practices into your galley.

A fire extinguisher should be mounted in plain sight but well away from the stove where the fire may prevent you from reaching it. All those who use the boat should be instructed in its use and made thoroughly familiar with its operation, thereby reducing panic and the possibility of mistakes in an emergency. The charge should be checked at least once a month.

A pound of baking soda is a good alternative: one pound thrown directly into the base of a twelve-inch diameter fire will usually put it out immediately. Baking soda is not as messy to clean up as the powder from a fire extinguisher, and is every bit as effective for a small fire. Using baking soda also saves the extinguisher for a more serious fire. Store it permanently beside the fire extinguisher, where it can be held in position with a shock cord. Have its plastic container clearly labeled in red.

A blanket is another alternative, and one should be stored near the galley. A heavy wool blanket placed over a blaze will starve it of oxygen and thus smother it. Wool is preferable because it doesn't burn as readily as cotton or synthetics, and can double up as a cozy wrap on cool evenings. If there is time to get water, a wet blanket works even better; alternatively, the fire can be covered with the blanket while water is being fetched. If the fire is large, a wet blanket can be thrown over its center and the perimeters doused with the fire extinguisher.

A boat afloat has access to great quantities of water, which is fine for alcohol fires or those which don't involve gasoline, kerosene or grease. But water does not mix with petroleum distillates, and when it is added to an oil fire the oil rises to the surface and continues to burn. Water may even cause oil fires to spread by splattering flaming droplets of oil to new areas, or by causing a contained oil fire to overflow onto the floor as it is displaced by the water. But for alcohol and non-petroleum fires, a gallon of water stored near the galley will cover such contingencies as uncharged fire extinguishers and missing blankets or baking soda. Water stored close to the galley is doubly necessary if cooking aboard is carried on during a haul-out.

All fuels should be stored someplace out of the galley where they cannot explode or make a large fire out of a small one. Because propane and gasoline fumes are heavier than air, tanks containing these fuels must be vented overboard and not into the galley or bilge. A remote control shutoff for the propane tank eliminates the possibility of a leak in the stove, provided, of course, it is turned off when the stove is not in use.

The fittings that lead from the storage tank to the stove should be inspected regularly to make sure they have not corroded, or twisted, or that a heavy object has not fallen on a line and caused damage. The fittings should be accessible for this visual inspection.

The alcohol required for pre-ignition of kerosene stoves should be stored at least twelve inches from the stove, and it should be in a holder that cannot tip over. A plastic squeeze container is a good idea; it allows exactly the right amount to be inserted. If it's poured straight from the bottle, a heavy sea (or a heavy hangover) can result in spillage.

When transferring fuels, a method that prevents spillage is advisable. Funnels help, but the best method I've seen for kerosene is an outboard motor gas line with priming bulb. Squeezing the bulb effortlessly siphons the kerosene from the storage tank to the stove, without losing a drop. If your stove is portable, it's a good idea to fill it in the cockpit where spilled fuel is more easily and more thoroughly cleaned up.

Matches should be kept in a metal or glass container well away from the stove. They can be largely avoided by using flint steels or metal strikers (acetylene lighters). However, neither of these will ignite alcohol.

A metal or glass container for dead matches, kept beside the stove, discourages still-warm matches from being put into the garbage where they may smoulder. The dead-match container is even preferable to throwing a match overboard, unless you're on deck and can see the match land in the water. A serious fire was once caused by a not-quite-extinguished match being tossed overboard from a boat interior. The match was caught in a back eddy of wind and landed in the midst of a line of clothing on deck, where it grew into quite a bonfire before anyone noticed it.

If the dead match container has an inch of water in it, it will double as an instant snuffer of chef's cigarettes.

Combustibles such as aerosol cans and flammables such as rum, vaseline, suntan lotions, and so on, should not be left near the stove or stored behind or above it.

There should be a good light over the galley, as poor lighting may cause bungling that can lead to fire.

If there are curtains in the galley, or anywhere near the stove, they should be fiberglass or some other nonflammable material. If you are not absolutely sure the fabric is nonflammable, it does not belong in the galley.

The galley floor should be nonskid. Urethaned teak and holly is pretty — pretty slippery when wet! It can cause lurching that ends in fire.

If there is an opening port in the galley, you should be able to close it from the exterior, as a fire in the galley may prevent you from reaching it.

The stove itself should be set in about twelve inches from the edge of the counter so that knobs cannot be accidentally turned on, and so that people brushing by will not have their hair or clothes catch on fire. I saw a shirt burst into flame once when a man stood for a moment with his back to the stove.

The stove should sit in a two or three-inch well, or the stove counter should be completely surrounded by a two or three-inch solid fiddle so that any fire caused by spillage of fuel will be contained.

The material both over and under the stove should be nonflammable, and that on the overhead should be either asbestos or asbestos-lined. Our experiments indicate that fire-retardant styrofoam often used in insulation doesn't burn any more slowly than untreated styrofoam; perhaps in volume it does.

If possible, there should be no stowage holds directly behind the stove, because inevitably one has to reach over the flame to get at them. This could cause a burn and a sudden movement which could result in a grease spill. The burn itself could be bad enough.

Safe galley habits will minimize the risk of fire. Never fill a hot stove. Do not fill pots so full that they boil over and extinguish a flame, leaving escaping gas to be exploded by a match or the other burner. Clean up grease spills immediately, even little ones. Grease used for deep frying should be poured as soon as possible into a storage container with a tight lid, and never left in an open pot as you might in a house. Watch over newcomers their first few times at the stove, even if they say they know how to operate it. We didn't once and regretted it. The scorched overhead was a constant reminder.

If, in spite of all precautions, fire should break out:
— call everyone to help;
— determine the nature of the fire and select appropriate fire-fighting methods and equipment;
— close all hatches, ports and doors;
— remove all flammables;
— if the fire appears to be getting out of hand, call the aid of other boaters in the area;
— check the dinghy for oars, life vests, water, anchor and line.

The following incident illustrates the necessity of having the dinghy prepared in advance in case of fire. Four years ago at Hogsty Reef in the Bahamas, five men leapt into a dinghy when a gasoline explosion made a blazing inferno of their boat. The dinghy lacked oars and anchor, however, and this oversight almost cost them their lives. Unable to anchor or row back to their anchorage, they drifted without water for five days until their dinghy chanced to wash up on an island some hundred miles downwind.

And here is an incident which shows the importance of having either sufficient space in the dinghy, or a sufficient number of dinghies to hold all the people on board. A few months ago in Florida a stove exploded on a forty-six-foot sailboat that carried nine children, varying in age from three months to fourteen years, and three adults. The fire was almost immediately out of control, yet all escaped safely in minutes in the boat's three dinghies.

In the final analysis, an emergency of any kind is the best handled when those involved have given thought to the possibility of disaster and prepared themselves as best they can. Many emergencies on a boat do not leave much time for thought — just seconds in some cases, minutes in others. The bulk of your clear-headed thinking and preparation must be done beforehand.

Chapter 3:
Water

"IF THEY DON'T IMPROVE THE QUALITY OF THIS WATER, I'M MOVING OUT !"

"Where do you get your water?" "My water's got funny brown things growing in it, do you think I should drink it?" "Can I borrow a gallon of water until I go ashore in the morning?" "We were getting low on water so we had to pull into port." "We cleaned out our water tanks this morning and you should see the slimy stuff in the bottom — it's a wonder we're not all dead!"

Sometimes it seems as if your whole life aboard revolves around water tanks and getting them filled. Perhaps that is not so strange when you consider that the major substance in the body is water, and you would die without it in a matter of days. Just ask your doctor.

Sailors are notorious, our doctor (also a sailor) told us, for drinking too little water. They are always trying to preserve their precious supply. Good health demands that you consume upwards of two quarts a day, unless you're in the tropics, in which case you should consume more than three. Ordinarily, the body loses two to three quarts a day through excretion and perspiration, but an active person in an arid environment can lose ten.

It would appear, then, that the old sea adage, "half a gallon per person per day," falls short. But until the nineteenth century, daily rations included a gallon of beer and a pint of wine. So in actual fact, yesterday's sailors probably consumed about a gallon and a half of liquid. However, while beer served pretty much the same function as water in the body, rum or strong wine might be stretching the point — they are dehydrating.

Sailors frequently suffer from maladies stemming from too small a water intake, salt depletion and kidney stones being the most common. Symptoms of salt depletion may include nausea, dizziness, exhaustion, vomiting, cramping in the legs or any muscles being used at the time, confusion, anxiety, depression. Water may make this condition worse — it merely dilutes the salts remaining in the body. What is needed at this point is salt (sodium chloride is the main one) in the form of a salt tablet or some very salty meals. The major symptom of kidney stones is pain in the side or groin, usually severe, but sometimes nagging. Medical attention should be shought immediately. Many stones can be avoided by religiously drinking three quarts every day. That's twelve eight-ounce glasses.

Be sure that your water storage is the best possible. Drinking three quarts a day won't do much good if the water is contaminated with bacteria or chemicals. Water tanks should be made of cured epoxy which is totally inert, or stainless steel which is almost completely so. Tanks should have a removable lid to facilitate cleaning once a year, and if larger than a twenty-five-gallon capacity, should be baffled to ensure against rupture when contents slosh violently. And not all the water should be stored in bilge tanks, in case of mishaps on rocks or reefs which could result in loss of the entire supply.

Plastic jerry jugs left in the cockpit will grow algae, although small amounts do not make the water unpotable. The jugs should be rinsed two or three times with fresh water before filling. Algae can mostly be removed by first shaking a handful of pebbles in the jug for several minutes, and then by allowing a solution of half water, half hydrochloric acid (one cupful or so) to sit in the jug for fifteen minutes. Never add water to acid, as it may splash; add acid to water. This also sterilizes.

Bleach will sterilize as well, but will not remove algae growth. Since it now appears that chlorine is carcinogenic, any jug that is treated with chlorine should be rinsed three times.

Your original source of water, of course, must be good. Do not assume that water from a tap is necessarily pure, as if the tap were a stamp of approval. Too many communities have been ordered not to drink the town water because of pollution from pesticides, chemicals or manure. Is there any safe water? In decreasing quantities, it seems. Bottled water is usually safe. Some boaters have purifiers in the galley, and this definitely provides good water, as long as the charcoal is regularly cleaned or replaced. Most city water is relatively okay, if you don't mind the chlorine and fluoride, both of which are now believed to be carcinogenic. Perhaps the French have found the answer — switch to wine.

For emergencies, if you must drink contaminated water in order to survive, a liter of water is made pure (of bacteria only, typhoid and diphtheria being the major concerns) with five Aqua-pura (halazone) tablets, or a few drops of bleach or iodine, and allowing it to sit for twenty minutes. Boiling for twenty minutes will also kill bacteria. If you go ocean sailing, there should be at least one saltwater still per person on board. And if you should ever find yourself adrift at sea in a lifeboat with a diminishing water supply, you can stretch it by adding twenty per cent salt water.

When the six of us were shipwrecked on Hogsty Reef, toward the end of our twelve-day stay with only ten gallons of water left, and not knowing when rescue would come, we considered stetching the water supply by adding one cup of sea water to every four fresh. We calculated this to be about the same salinity as blood, and therefore the saltiest water the body could endure for a prolonged period. I have since read in a survival manual that this is so.

With good water becoming a somewhat scarce commodity and many towns installing water meters and charging appropriately, and because getting water on board can be a problem at times, it is a good practice to use as little as possible.

These are some ways in which boaters can conserve water: Brush teeth in half a glass of water. Do most cooking with a pressure cooker, as it reduces water consumption by as much as eighty per cent. Water used for rinsing sprouts can be saved and used for soups, sauces, or for the dog to drink. If you are on the ocean, fifty per cent salt water can be used for cooking, but I don't know if I'd use Great Lakes water with the mercury and dioxin levels still in dispute. But do use salt or lake water for all washing. Get double use out of wash water by using it first to wash something not too dirty, say blouses, and then for something dirtier, like the floor. Use only four cups of water, instead of a whole sinkful, for washing dishes — this is not enough to immerse plates in, but when used in a deep bowl it is adequate for sloshing soapy water over dishes and getting them clean. A gravity-fed hose with fine spray for rinsing dishes uses a minimum of water, less than a cupful for dishes of four. A whistling tea kettle will help keep water from boiling away (if you heed the whistle).

Label all recycled containers to avoid disastrous consequences. We once sailed on a boat that used old bleach jugs to store their water. A swimmer came aboard, his eyes smarting from the salt water, and dashed some of this "water" into his eyes — only it wasn't water, it was bleach brought up temporarily from the bilge for a cleaning job. We all screamed at him to jump overboard. Horrified, he threw himself back into the water. There were no ill effects, and we were amazed and thankful.

In summary, then, these points are most important: Drink plenty of liquid. Make sure the original source of water is good. Use water tanks that have removable lids. Store water elsewhere than in bilge tanks. Kill bacteria with bleach, halazone or iodine, or by boiling for twenty minutes. Stretch water by adding twenty per cent salt water.

Concern over drinking water is nothing new to boaters. Water is everything to them. Be it blue, green, white, salt, fresh, turbid, clear, good or bad, they are probably more conscious of its preciousness and infinite varieties than any other segment of the population. Yet they must be on guard at all times to conserve, protect, and use it wisely.

Chapter 4:
Coping with a Small Galley

Unless you were born a Spartan, preparing meals in what seems to be a peewee-sized galley may turn your customary chuckles into snarls in a matter of seconds. When the crew carts eight bags of groceries into the cockpit, you can only glare at them — where on earth do they think you're going to stow it all? And when some old boating friends troop down the dock to see you at lunch time, you panic — how can you prepare sandwiches for ten people on a two-square-inch counter?

It's true that after years of working in a kitchen which you can *walk* around in, life does take some getting used to in a galley that you can barely *turn* around in. But you will, and you will revel in the efficiency of the small space.

Three basic habits should be acquired.

One: Clean up as you go. A dirty pot, or even something as small as a dirty knife, takes up a portion of your valuable counter space. Wash it, and get it out of the way. This is also a practice which stands you in good stead for a long offshore passage — the last thing you want when rough weather hits suddenly is dirty dishes sliding around.

Two: Avoid buying anything that is heavily packaged. Not only do these items take up excess space in your cupboards before they are consumed, but you must deal with them once they become garbage. And large green bags of garbage on a small boat are a plebeian pain!

Three: Avoid buying prepared foods which are more space-consuming than the same product in its basic, or raw, state. For example, buy the popping corn kernels rather than the already popped corn — not only is it cheaper, it's fresher. Buy regular rice rather than minute rice — it takes only five minutes to cook in a pressure cooker. And dried beans will take up far less space than their tinned equivalents. No, they're *not* a lot of trouble. Just soak overnight: bring to fifteen pounds pressure when the stove is going for breakfast; again at lunch; and by supper time they are ready. A total of about two minutes of your time.

Here are more space-saving ideas:

Kettle holder: This brilliant idea was conceived by Jim Brown, designer of the Searunner series of trimarans. Because a kettle is perhaps the most space-consuming item in the galley (other pots cannot be stored inside it), to have it stored out of the cupboard liberates a good deal of space. The type of kettle you need has a protruding rim around the bottom. It is this rim that slides into the kettle holder that you make for it. The kettle can then be slipped into the holder, which is on the bulkhead.

Here is how to make it — glue and nail together these three pieces of plywood:

— ¼" plywood about 4" wider than diameter of kettle

A. backboard

—same thickness as rim on bottom of kettle
—diameter is same as that of rim

B. spacer

— ¼" plywood, finished decoratively
—diameter is same as diameter of kettle above rim

C. finish plate

—rim which slides into slot between A and C

D. kettle

Cooler built in to fit the shape of the hull: This cooler will, of course, be narrow at the bottom and flare out toward the top at the back side as the hull broadens. If money is no object, have the basic unit welded out of stainless steel, leaving room for two to four inches of closed cell polyurethane foam for insulation all around it. Or simply lay two layers of six-ounce glass over the foam (that has been previously cut to shape and glued in place) with epoxy resin. Do not use polyester resin as it leaves an odor that will taint food.

The drain hole can lead outside if the whole cooler is above the water line. Or it can lead into a jug in the bilge which is periodically emptied. So as not to interfere with counter space, but still have the cooler top-opening to retain as much cold air as possible, make sure the lid is flush with the counter. The ring you grasp to pull the lid open can be sunk flush with its surroundings too.

Sink, and a small one at that: The double sink used to be many a modern woman's idea of luxury. It has now become almost standard equipment. But by no stretch of the imagination can it be called essential. The same with a large sink — you don't need it to be larger than your largest plate. Both the second sink and the large sink are colossal wasters of counter space.

Sink cover: Regardless of the size of your sink, a cover made to be flush with the counter is a marvelous thing. Granted, there are times when you need the whole sink when preparing a meal, but usually what you need is more counter space. This cover gives you not only the extra space of the cover itself, but also converts into usable space those two or three inches behind or beside the sink that would otherwise have been too small to be considered part of the working counter.

If made out of hardwood such as mahogany, the bottom side can be left unpainted and will double as a cutting board. A finger-sized hole is cut into it for easy removal. And a larger hole may be cut under the tap so that water can be run through while the cover is in place.

Sliding doors: In the narrow walkway that may be part of your galley, cupboard doors that swing to open may be awkward and irritating. A sliding door requires no swing space. And furthermore, when closed it does not need to be locked to prevent things from falling out when you are slamming into six-foot waves.

Knifeholder: This may sound like a trivial item, but it accomplishes four things. It keeps all the knives out of harm's way. It clears some of the clutter out of the utensil drawer. It prevents knife edges from getting dulled or knicked. And it makes good use of the otherwise unused space on the back of a cupboard door. The best design I have seen is also the simplest: a strip of leather tacked at various intervals, and the knives are slid through the spaces between the tacks or screws.

Square containers and jars: A square container occupies less space than a round one, and has the added advantage in heavy weather of not rolling around, producing maddening clinks, when you are trying to get some sleep before it's your watch again. When it falls it stays put. The ten-ounce Nescafé jars are perfect.

No oven: How often do you really use an oven? And how often when you have used it, could you have used the top of the stove instead? I would wager that, on most boats, the number of times the oven is used does not justify the space it occupies. Experiment with the top of the stove. Very few, if any, are the recipes that cannot be adapted from oven to stove top.

Net bags: These bags can be hung in unused overhead space, and will hold a variety of things, from fruits and vegetables, to clothes, to charts, to children's toys, to lifejackets.

Keep the galley equipment to a minimum: Avoid bringing aboard utensils or pots that have only one use, for example, a garlic press or an egg poacher. Many of these items are, after all, just gadgets. Garlic can be adequately pressed with the flat side of a knife, and eggs can be nicely poached in a small pot of boiling water.

I never cease to wonder at the compactness and efficiency of a galley. Everything is within arm's reach. Stowage for every item must be carefully thought out. Anyone who knows me will say that I don't exactly ooze domesticity when ashore, and that I'm not too particular about what goes on in the kitchen. But put me on board my boat and I become quite fanatical about what goes where. I am intrigued by the fact that the compact galley is part of a specialized way of life that demands neatness, precision and smallness for survival.

Chapter 5:
Choosing Galley Ware

It just doesn't work to transport pots and plates to the boat every time you want to sail, as if you were going on a picnic. Sailing is often an impromptu thing — you won't want to go home first and pick up the cooking gear. And you can never remember everything you need. In addition, what you use at home is not necessarily ideal for use on the boat. Your boat should be ready to go at all times, with its own specifically chosen items.

Factors you will want to keep in mind when selecting the galley ware are: breakability, safety, ease of use, ease of cleaning, space occupied and possible health hazards. And you will want to steer clear of nonessentials, choosing whenever possible to use gear that fills more than one function.

If you cook without much fanfare and for only a few people the least you can get by on is a frying pan, a pressure cooker, and one other smaller pot, perhaps the one-quart size. However, individual needs are different. We know a single-hander on a small boat who does all his cooking in a frying pan, and a woman who cooks for her family of eleven with three pressure cookers and nothing else.

Don't pick a pot with a round handle. There are times on a boat when it's hard to steady a full, heavy pot, and a round handle is tough to get a good grip on . The handle should be flattened or rectangular, and it should be long, rather than two little lips on either side of the pot. A pot that required two hands to lift it is hard to manage on a boat, where you often need one hand to steady yourself. Besides, these lips get too hot for bare hands, and then you have to hunt for the pot holders. Such a pot is a potential hazard.

Similarly, the lid should have a handle that does not conduct heat so that, once again, you don't have to search for a pot holder.

Be sure the pot has a tight fitting lid — the locking lid of the pressure cooker is ideal. Even if you don't plan to familiarize yourself with the numerous advantages of pressure cooking, your primary pot on the boat should be a pressure cooker because of this single safety feature. It prevents meals from getting lost, and people from getting burned. (More about the pressure cooker in Chapter 6.)

Because the source of heat on a boat is almost invariably a flame, all the pots should have thick bottoms such as cast iron or cast aluminum to reduce the chance of burning. Aluminum spreads heat more quickly and evenly than stainless steel, but heavy stainless steel pots now often have cast aluminum bottoms welded onto them. These are perfect for the boat. They are durable, easy to clean, don't stain or rust, and always look good.

Pots made entirely of cast aluminum are fine, too, but they do stain. And lately there have been reports that aluminum pots are responsible for intestinal upsets caused by the ingestion of bits of aluminum being scraped into the food. Aluminum is not biodegradable; it is possible that minute bits can become lodged here and there and cause problems. If this is so, use only wooden utensils in aluminum pots, and do not use metal pot scrubbers, thereby reducing the quantity of aluminum that is scraped off.

An aluminum pot will corrode in salt water, but I have found that this can be avoided by rinsing the pot in a bit of freshwater after washing with sea water. However, the rusting of cast iron cannot be controlled in this way. The pot will disintegrate before your eyes, with huge flakes popping off the bottom. You can get around this problem by using the various makes of cast iron that are coated inside and out with enamel, such as Creuset pots from France, or Dansk pots. These are very serviceable, very attractive and very expensive. If you should decide to splurge on one of these pots, choose a dark blue or brown rather than a light color, as stains will look less offensive, even kind of homey, on a dark color.

If your boat is tiny, you should consider not having a kettle. It is a very space-consuming item. In this case, be sure that one of your pots has a pouring lip so that boiling water can be transferred safely into a cup. Or you can use a two-cup aluminum teapot or coffee pot. They're very small. But a kettle is a far safer way to boil water on a boat — if you regularly have even one hot drink a day, hunt for a small kettle.

If you do choose the full-size kettle, it should be the whistling variety. The whistle ensures that the stove (always a potential fire hazard) need not be on a moment longer than necessary. And should the kettle topple in a choppy sea, less of the scalding liquid will escape, for the cover over the spout will contain most of it. Finally, stainless steel kettles are easier to clean than aluminum ones.

Plates are a problem. Plastic gets scruffy looking after a few months. Earthenware always looks good, but it is heavy, bulky, and breakable. China, although not bulky, is also breakable. We have a friend who uses wooden plates, and after four years he's still happy with the choice. But I find them cumbersome and tedious to wash, and they take up a lot of space in the cupboard. Paper plates are not too tedious to wash, but you have to keep replacing them and they leak. They also add to your mound of garbage.

We finally settled on sturdy enamel plates which have a flared 3/4" high rim. The depth is excellent for containing a sloppy meal. I was apprehensive when I brought them home, thinking they might look campish, because they were deep red, but on the wood hues of our plank table they looked wonderful.

Buy glasses that stack — they will have to be plastic. If you think plastic looks cheap and crummy, shop at some of the gift shops which carry a better line of plastic glasses. The plastic may still look crummy to you, but it certainly will not be *cheap.*

Don't buy special salad bowls. The traditional thick wood salad bowls take up a lot of your valuable cupboard space, are extra trouble to wash, and usually too shallow to be used for other purposes. As such, they're a frivolous item and don't belong in the efficient galley. Instead, choose soup bowls that can double as salad and small serving bowls. There is an attractive, thin, lightweight, woven wood bowl with plastic finish made in Taiwan that sells for about sixty cents in hardware and department stores. It is nonbreakable, easy to wash, multipurpose, and stacks well in a small space.

All these pots, dishes and glasses should be stowed so that they don't roll around when the boat is underway. To keep these and other items such as canned goods from sliding, line the shelves with a non-skid surface. There is a rubber-like webbed mat that works well available by the foot at hardware stores.

Restrain yourself when it comes to buying galley ware. If there are usually two and occasionally four, don't buy dishes for six. On the very rare occasion that you may be feeding more than four, the extra people can make do with a mug, or other item. Part of boating is making do.

Breakable items are to be avoided on a boat for two reasons. Broken glass is always dangerous, but it is even more so when the boat is lurching and you can't be sure of your footing. Any accidents that disable crew members when you're out sailing will jeopardize the safety of the boat and all aboard. And broken items are not easily replaceable when you're boating. If you're in the middle of the Atlantic, or just beginning a two-week cruise in the Thousand Islands and you break your only mixing bowl, then you just have to do without.

However, when it comes to wine glasses, we feel justified in ignoring our rule about breakable items in the galley. We just cannot properly appreciate wine in anything but a wine glass. So I'm always buying wine glasses, because they are always breaking (but that's okay, because I enjoy buying wine glasses!). We've tried drinking wine from silver goblets, pewter and brass, but we don't like what the metals do to the wine. So if you feel as we do, keep wine glasses in a rack in an out-of-the-way spot, to reduce breakage. Or you can wrap each glass in a tea towel or wash cloth and keep them in a bin with other light things.

Depending on the type of cooking you enjoy and the amount of space you have, you can broaden your range of ware with such items as a wok, a fondue pot, a toaster, a griddle iron, and so on.

You can even have a blender — far away from the convenience of dockside power. However, we know one couple who used a blender extensively on land, and didn't want to compromise their good meals even for a two-week holiday. Their solution required an outboard, and a certain kind of blender which has a square adapter on the bottom (such as an Osterizer). They welded a matching square male fitting on to the very center of the fly wheel, placed the blender on this adapter, and held it thereby while the engine was started, run for a minute or two, and then shut down. When the blades stopped turning, the blender full of frothy goodness was removed.

Galleys are very personal — but they all have some limitations and problems in common. Before putting together your own galley, you should discuss it with as many experienced boaters as possible. But the most important thing is to select galley gear with your own special needs in mind. And be sure it is safe.

To use such equipment, so purposefully chosen, will be a pleasure.

Chapter 6:
The Pressure Cooker

A few years ago, near Toronto, a large, newly-launched boat burned beyond repair and sank. The owners were ashore for a few minutes while a pot of potatoes boiled over and put out the propane flame under the pot. Gas escaping from the extinguished burner was ignited by the flame in the other burner, and there was an explosion. Several gallons of gasoline stored nearby made short work of the boat.

This tragedy would not have happened had the pot in use been a pressure cooker. The amount of water used in a pressure cooker is very small, usually no more than a half cup. By the time the contents of the pot are raised to twenty pounds pressure — the point at which the safety valve releases and sprays the deckhead with your supper — all the water will have been converted to steam. The burner flame cannot be extinguished. For this reason alone the pressure cooker qualifies as safety equipment aboard a boat.

This is one dramatic demonstration of the value of a pressure cooker. There are many other reasons why we would not be without two of these marvelous pots on our boat.

Water and fuel must be conserved on any boat. Instead of four or five cups of water for a potfull of vegetables, a half cup is all that is needed. This has the further advantage of saving vitamins and water-soluble minerals, which are not leeched out in cooking. And instead of the half hour the burner would be on to cook a pot of brown rice, eight minutes is enough. Less fuel is consumed.

Another valuable commodity saved by the pressure cooker is the cook's time. The cook will spend about one-third the time at the stove. And the time saved can mean the difference between a poor and a well-balanced diet. Most men forced to cook on a boat, if given the choice between boiling carrots for thirty minutes and grabbing another slice of bread to have with their steak, will choose the bread. But if they knew that the pressure cooker could have the carrots ready in six minutes flat, they might choose the carrots as part of a better diet.

Also if you are accustomed to spending so much time in the galley that you miss out on most of the sailing, or are just too tired to take an interest, a pressure cooker or two will give you the extra time to enjoy the water rushing past the hull.

Pressure cookers can double as ovens, so the large amount of space usually taken by an oven is liberated for other things. True, a folding oven does not occupy much space if you indeed fold it (some owners of folding ovens leave them assembled for convenience), but it is a hassle. "Oven" recipes and methods for pressure cookers can be found in many cookbooks and in the booklets that come with the cooker.

Whether or not your stove is gimballed, there are times when pots have the uncanny ability to perform gymnastic impossibilities on, and off, the top of the stove. At such times, the locking lid of the pressure cooker is a real boon. You can bash to windward for days (if you really must!) and the lid will not bounce off the pot, the soup will not slop over the top, and the chili will not fly around the cabin when the pot leaps off the stove.

One day while slamming into seas and forty knots of wind along the north coast of Haiti, we met up with a particularly aggressive crest of water, and the pressure cooker, full of stew, crashed to the floor. This having never happened to me before, I watched with horror and expected at least a minor explosion. But nothing happened. And not a drop leaked out. With an ordinary pot this would have been a disaster. At the very least we would have been slithering about in slippery stew and someone might have been seriously scalded. As it was, I merely reached down, retrieved the errant cooker and asked the captain if he was ready for some hot stew.

This same feature, the locking lid, makes the pressure cooker ideal for carting prepared food ashore for a beach picnic with no danger of it capsizing in the bottom of the dinghy, or of the lid sliding off into five fathoms of water while you watch it glide to its final resting place.

Pressure cookers are made of either aluminum or stainless steel. The stainless steel ones have a cast aluminum bottom for a more even distribution of heat. And because of their thickness, they retain heat for long periods of time. This means that the cook need not to panic about getting everything ready and hot for the right moment of serving. A pot of rice, for example, will stay hot in a pressure cooker for almost an hour; it can be prepared well in advance and forgotten until the meal is ready to go on the table. The thickness of these pots also ensures that a pot of food destined for the beach, if hot when it left the boat, will still be hot by the time the fish have been grilled over the driftwood fire.

Having a pressure cooker aboard makes possible a valuable addition to your cooking: canning. If you are able to can, you needn't be dependent on the limited selection of tinned foods that you find on the grocery shelf in small out-of-the-way harbors. You will own turkey, beef chuck, beef heart, chicken livers, hamburger or spaghetti sauce, and meals at sea will become much more interesting with less risk to health.

Being able to can also means that when you catch a forty-pound tuna or an eighty-pound turtle, it is no longer necessary to discard the excess when you can't eat it all. You just can it. We have canned excess conch too, which is well-known for its toughness — the canning process renders it very tender so that it is almost like Nova Scotia scallops. Other people have canned lobster, and sailing friends of ours once even canned a goat they had caught.

Canning is one more skill on the road to self-sufficiency. And self-sufficiency is probably the basic drive that motivates every man or woman who has ever yearned to go to sea in a small boat.

It is evident that several of the uses for pressure cookers are money-savers. But what about the expense of the cooker itself? The $40, or the $120 for the big pressure cooker-canner, is a staggering sum, especially when you are still reeling from forking over a pile of money for the gallon of bottom paint. But who says you have to buy a brand-new one? I bought my four-quart cooker at a flea market for a dollar, and it worked perfectly. And my cooker-canner only cost six dollars at a Goodwill store. Nothing on it worked, but for an additional $8, the company that made that particular brand was able to put it in A-1 condition. It is definitely the most useful and versatile galley tool on our boat.

In my opinion (and that of the skipper, who uses it as routinely as I do), the pressure cooker is as basic to life aboard a small boat as fishing gear or a fire extinguisher.

Today, I'd be lost without one even on land.

Chapter 7:
Who Needs Ovens?

For three years I cooked on a two-burner kerosene stove, often preparing three meals a day for eight to ten people. I discovered, through feasts and flops, that there is nothing an oven can do that top-of-the-stove can't handle just as well.

When we first launched *Isla*, we had absolutely no spare cash for such amenities as an oven. "I can make do temporarily," I grumbled. "Meanwhile we'll keep our eyes open for an oven, secondhand ...."

I love to cook. I love trying new things. And living aboard full time, often out of reach of grocery stores and native markets, puts you squarely at the mercy of your own initiative and inventiveness.

While sitting at anchor in the beautiful, calm, isolated bay at Little Harbour on Long Island in the Bahamas, reveling in the peace and solitude of the place after a battering beat from Rum Cay, the idea leaped to mind: Pizza! I must have pizza!

But how, with no oven on board? What to do? The frying pan! I rolled the dough, laid it in the pan going up the sides half an inch, spread on some spiced-up tomato paste, chopped onions, and salami (bought six months before), and crowned it with cheese. With the lid on, I "baked" it for about twenty minutes over medium heat using a flame tamer (a square sheet of asbestos or aluminum, or anything not flammable, to spread the heat) under the pan. The pizza was terrific!

With the success of experiments like this one, we were no longer on the lookout for an oven. In fact, I definitely did not want one. The advantages would be too few to make up for the problems an oven creates — storage, taking up space, maintenance and excess heat, especially on nights when the Aladdin lamp is already chasing everyone topside. Furthermore, after visiting Haiti and the Dominican Republic where women cook for large families on a single charcoal burner, I look upon my two-burner as a luxury.

The ways in which the stove top can substitute for an oven are many and varied.

Yeast and soda breads can be made in the pressure cooker — without pressure — using flame tamers. Sprinkle cornmeal or poppy seeds in the greased pressure cooker to prevent burning.

Steamed bread (the date-nut loaf or Boston brown bread type) can be done either for two hours in a large pot half filled with simmering water, or for thirty minutes at fifteen pounds pressure in a pressure cooker. Just pour the batter into greased molds (empty tin cans) to the halfway point, and use foil to cover the top. The *Joy of Cooking* and *Mother Earth News #42* have some super recipes for steamed breads.

I prepare cakes, muffins, and brownies in a greased frying pan with a light sprinkling of cornmeal. The pan is covered, and placed on two flame tamers. The muffin I make — a single, big round "turnover" — can be flipped to brown the top, something the ladies on Rum Cay have been doing for two years. And I thought I'd invented it!

Casseroles do nicely in a pressure cooker (without pressure) or in any heavy cast iron pot over medium heat with two flame tamers. Paprika sprinkled on top will give them a crispy look.

Roasts can be sliced two-and-a-half to three inches thick, sprinkled with meat tenderizer and cooked about twenty minutes over medium heat with one flame tamer. Even cheap cuts are delicious like this. And meat loaf ingredients can be pressed into a loaf shape, wrapped (or not) in aluminum foil and laid in a frying pan with the lid on. Just use low heat, and one flame tamer.

My pie shells are baked in a pie plate which fits into my large pressure cooker-canner. The plate sits on a rack which keeps it a good two inches from the bottom of the cooker. It takes half an hour to cook at high heat. A sixty-second, heavenly, unbaked filling consists of one can of sweetened condensed milk with half a cup of freshly-squeezed lime juice stirred into it — presto, *Key Lime Pie.*

The only kind of pie I have tried that calls for baked filling is pumpkin pie (for which the skipper has a passion). I simply perch the pie plate on a rack almost two inches off the bottom of the frying pan; at medium heat, baking takes forty-five minutes. Excess filling can be processed as a semi-custard in tin cans in the pressure cooker at fifteen pounds pressure for seven minutes.

Custard takes only three minutes at fifteen pounds pressure in one large mold; or you can position several small molds in the pressure cooker. But custard can also be done, like the steamed breads, in a pot of simmering water for half an hour or so.

And Welsh cakes, a special recipe, are delicious, nutritious, a little different, and particularly well-adapted to the frying pan. (See index.)

For the past year we have been leading a land-bound existence. Because I found stove-top cooking on the boat so simple and such a time and fuel saver, I have used the oven only twice during the entire year spent in this house. Roasting twenty-pound turkeys is the only thing I have not figured out how to do on top of the stove.

Otherwise, who needs ovens?

Chapter 8:
Sailing without Refrigeration

What sort of dementia induces otherwise normal boaters to lead their life afloat without refrigeration, or at the very least, ice? And is it contagious?

Those with mild symptoms have been smitten with the KISS (Keep it Simple, Stupid) variety. Basically, these boaters want to avoid the frustration of having to deal with systems that break down. A breakdown, they realize, may involve (a) hours of intricate repairs, (b) weeks of waiting for some special part, (c) a good chunk of the cruising fund, (d) ulcers, (e) all of the above. And these people who do not have refrigeration systems have absolutely no trouble with them.

Not having to worry about imminent or actual breakdowns leaves boaters' minds free to pursue more pleasurable paths ... which makes them vulnerable to the second and more serious of the two varieties of dementia: KIMM (Keep It Mellow, Mate). Top priority for these people is peace. And every jarring thing that might intrude upon the rich harmony they are aiming for is avoided — such as a noisy, smelly generator that requires maintenance and would interfere with the gentle sounds of Nature; or such as spending money on nonessentials (refrigerator, radar, and so on) that would require them to interrupt their chosen lifestyle to make the money to buy these things.

While adhering to the KIMM principle requires constant vigilance over your state of mind, following the KISS principle requires only that you reject the basic tenet of Western civilization, "bigger is better". Bigger refrigerators that hold larger supplies of ready-to-eat foods are NOT better when you end up losing (and wasting) hundreds of dollars of frozen food when the *#%! things break down. And they're certainly not better than the thrill of growing your own sprouts or gathering wild seabeans and periwinkles on the shore. Bigger quantities of fuel (to run the generator to keep the ice) are NOT better when you have to stay within reach of marinas to buy more fuel — and certainly not better than the joy of knowing you are living as economically as you can.

Okay, the decision has been made. No fridge, no ice. Now what? How do you go about making three meals a day for weeks on end without compromising variety and good nutrition?

Of all the things mentioned here, there are two that contribute more to self-sufficiency than all the rest put together. They are sprouts, and dried beans. Indeed, their usage would greatly enhance the diets even of those who do have cooling systems.

Sprouts are the answer to having a never-ending supply of fresh vegetables. They are crisp, tasty, contain ten times as much of vitamins A, B and C as spinach, and are easy and fun to grow. If allowed to grow a day or two past the pure sprout stage, tiny, nourishing green leaves appear, adding color and chlorophyl enzymes to the diet. Sprouts can be used in sandwiches, as a base or a garnish for soups, salads and egg foo yong, or fried alone or with other greens you may happen to have. They offer great variety to menus, as almost any seed can be sprouted, and every one looks and tastes different. And you don't have to pay exorbitant prices for them in health food stores. Buy mung beans (the chop suey type sprout) at half the price in Chinese markets. Buy lentils, lima beans, and so on in regular grocery stores — just read the package to be sure they haven't been treated with dangerous chemicals. Try sweet alfalfa, or nutty fenugreek (one of the basic seasonings in curry powder).

Dried beans (peas and lentils, too): There are three amazing things about dried beans. 1) They keep forever if moisture is kept out of their containers. 2) In combination with some grains, they form a complete protein. This gives you an alternative to the traditional sources of whole protein — meat, fish or fowl. For example, a bean and grain combination that we love is a Cuban dish called Congri, which is black beans and rice flavored with cumin and cayenne and a wee bit of bacon grease. (For a complete discussion of complementary proteins, read *Diet for a Small Planet* by Frances Moore Lappé.) 3) Dried beans can be delicious, and methods of preparation are almost limitless (try mashed kidney beans topped with melted cheese). And, of course, all the beans you carry with you can double as sprouts.

If your beans have sprouted slightly you can still make nourishing breads and soups. And they won't take as long to cook at this stage.

On a boat, dried beans are perfect — less heavy and less space-consuming than their tinned counterparts. And you don't have to worry about botulism from rusting tins. Two or three bay leaves will scare off any bugs.

Dried fruit is better for you than tinned, and it takes up less space. Good to eat as is, it can also be stewed, or chopped up to use in muffins or fruit breads. If you are away from stores, dry your own. I keep a supply of sun-dried Ontario elderberries. A cruising friend, I was amazed to hear, has dried *whole* oranges — the peel gets very leathery, he says, but the juice inside stays tangy for at least three months.

Dried vegetables also have greater nutritive value than their tinned equivalents, and offer additional variety — dried green peppers, for example. (They're no substitute for the crisp, fresh ones, but they are great for cooking.)

Freeze-dried fruits and vegetables are more expensive than the sun-dried or sulphur-cured varieties, but some people find the flavor so much better that the cost is worth it.

Meat: Bacterial growth on fresh meat can be retarded by a liberal sprinkling of salt — just wash it off before using the meat. Or you may prefer the many varieties of tinned meat that are available. Tinned bacon is great (if you don't mind carcinogens) and is available in some delicatessens and grocery stores — sometimes a grocery store will order in a quantity on special request. And canning your own gives you high-quality, low-cost meats in a greater variety than the supermarkets can offer.

Excess fish can be canned, smoked, or sun-dried, marinated in lime juice (called ceviche, pronounced "seveechee".) The fish looks and tastes cooked but it is not.

The most superb fishcakes I have ever tasted were made from the dried flesh of a large fish that had been drying in the rigging for a week. It was first scored about every inch to encourage it to dry rather than rot. I simply reconstituted it with water and a bit of lime juice, added flour, onions and spices, et voilà!

Excess conch is easy. Just put it, live, in a net, and drop it over the side. It can be kept for months like this, as the conch will keep on feeding while in the net.

Green hamburger will not kill you. Fry the hell out of it and make a spicier-than-usual chili.

Salad dressing: Here is a recipe that will not go bad: 1 can sweetened, condensed milk, ¼ cup vinegar, ¼ cup water, 1 teaspoon salt, and 2 teaspoons dry mustard. Mix until thickened.

Nuts contain oils which go rancid if the nuts are stored without the shells. Unshelled brazil nuts taste "off" after a few weeks. Make sure the shells have a good seal.

Bread: On special request, a bakery will double bake your bread. This puts a very hard crust on it which keeps it from going stale or moldy for about two weeks. After that, make your own. White flour will keep for months in airtight containers, but the oils in whole-wheat flour will go rancid in a month or so. The answer here is to carry the whole grain (which keeps for years) in airtight containers and grind a quantity as you need it. It takes about half an hour to grind enough for a week's use.

Cheese: Buy an entire round of cheese to be sure you are starting off with unexposed, uncontaminated cheese. Cut it up into pound chunks, or the amount you would use in one week, place it in a container and completely cover with cooking oil. It will keep at least six months. The cheese-flavored oil becomes a gourmet cook's delight.

Cottage cheese: Making your own is easy. Allow milk (reconstituted powdered) to sit until it curdles. Heat gently to solidify the curds, and strain off the whey. Season to taste.

Yogurt: Make your own, using a thermos to keep the temperature at a constant 110 degrees or so. Start off with live culture from fresh yogurt (2 tablespoons per quart of milk), or from a dormant culture in powdered form available in health food stores or dairies.

Eggs don't need any refrigeration if you want to keep them for only a few weeks. Smeared with vaseline they last about three months. Immersed in sodium silicate ("waterglass", available in drugstores) they last up to six months. You must buy fresh, unrefrigerated eggs to get the longest life out of them.

Jello: Agar-agar is a type of gelatin made from seaweed of that name, and it sets in an hour without refrigeration. Health food stores carry it.

Drinks: Did you know that ice-cold beverages (or ice-cold anything) anesthesize the taste buds and prevent you from savoring the full flavor of what you are drinking? One of the compensations, then, of drinking your beverages at room temperature is that you experience nuances of flavor you were never aware of before.

You can cool a bottle of wine to about twenty degrees below air temperature by wrappig a wet towel around it a good two hours before you want to use it. The process of evaporation requires heat, which it gets from the warm contents inside the bottle.

In summary, life on board without refrigeration (by choice, not by mishap) is neither a hardship nor a deprivation. On the contrary, it opens doors to unexplored horizons.

*   *   *

Chapter 9:
Cut Your Consumption of Galley Fuel

Alcohol, kerosene, gasoline, propane — they are all more expensive this year than they were last, and next year they won't be any cheaper.

On a small boat, the storage tanks for any of these fuels take up a big chunk of the already limited space. But fuels are an extreme fire hazard, so the less you carry on board, the smaller your risk of being blown to smithereens. Whatever the size of the tank, it seems as though you are always running low on fuel. And running out in the middle of the lake, or in the middle of a batch of pancakes, can be a big bore that dredges up interesting expletives your friends never thought you knew. On the ecological side, the less we use of these limited resources, the more there will be for everyone.

For all these reasons it is a worthwhile endeavor to curb our consumption of all fuels, the galley being a prime target.

Stove-top cooking is an easily-learned art which uses far less fuel than oven cooking. It dovetails nicely with such other shipboard ideals as liberating space (that an oven would occupy) for more essential items, spending less time in the galley (because food cooks faster on top of the stove than in the oven), and reducing the temperature in the galley. A three-inch thick roast of beef can be done to perfection in a frying pan, lid on, in twenty minutes. Rolls and biscuits can be cooked in about ten minutes in a frying pan and flipped to brown. Casseroles such as macaroni and cheese, Spanish rice, beef Stroganoff, mulligan, and scalloped potatoes are ready to eat in fifteen minutes in a thick-bottomed pot.

It is true that the absence of an oven will decrease the variety of meal preparation — at first. You just cannot have a baked potato, or brown the top of your casserole. But very soon, the creativity forced upon you by your "handicap" blossoms and the quality of meals soars. Because you are not doing things by the book, creativity becomes a way of life in the galley and the potential for variety is actually much greater.

If you absolutely must have an oven, consider a *folding one* that uses a burner, as this will use less fuel (and less space) than a regular oven.

The *pressure cooker* cuts back dramatically on fuel because steam heat under pressure makes food tender in much less time than dry heat. It also uses considerably less water, another precious shipboard commodity. A small chicken takes twenty minutes instead of two hours; custard, three minutes instead of an hour; white rice, four minutes instead of twenty-five; brown rice, eight minutes instead of forty-five. The list is long.

The *thermos* is essential to any galley that is serious about cutting down on fuel. It takes less fuel to boil six cups of water in one fell swoop than it does to heat six cups separately. And the thermos can be used as a kind of Dutch oven. For example, if you place one cup of rice and two cups of boiling water in the thermos in the morning, it will be ready for supper. The wide-mouthed thermos is preferable so that the contents can be easily removed.

A *whistling tea kettle* belongs in the energy-conscious galley, for it ensures that not one drop of fuel more than necessary is used to boil water.

Planning to have *one meal a day that requires no cooking* can cut down your fuel consumption by as much as one third. And because these are usually simple, no-fuss meals, it will give cook a break.

You need a back log of no-cook menus for this. For breakfast there is always cold cereal. But how about an egg nog, or fruit and a roll? A favorite of ours is cottage cheese with maple syrup dribbled over it. A friend has yogurt with honey stirred into it. Lunch is easy with sandwiches, or coleslaw with a cup of finely-chopped brazil nuts or almonds tossed in for protein. For supper, try a plate of cold cuts with tomatoes, or a plate of raw vegetables (cauliflower, broccoli, carrot sticks) with the rest of the chicken you had hot last night, or a wine and cheese party. A tasty and tender dish called ceviche (mentioned in the previous chapter) is raw fish marinated in lemon or lime juice. After an hour of exposure to the acid, the flesh becomes white and flakey, and looks cooked. The fish should be cut up into bite-sized pieces for marinating.

We sailed for a while on a boat where lunch was always a get-your-own affair — fast and easy. There were sandwich-making ingredients available like cheese, sprouts, onions, and so on. And it was the responsibility of the last person who ate to put everything away. This system resulted in the near-trampling to death of some of us, as the others would grab their food and bolt out the companionway in a mad effort not to be the last in the galley. Great fun, and it kept the stove in the background.

Consider *not having a fridge*. It gobbles fuel and space, and is just one more thing to maintain. It costs money, causes hassles and sometimes spoils food and even your disposition. See Chapter 8 for some details on how to set up the ship without refrigeration.

Good galley habits will help reduce the amount of fuel used. Cook twice the quantity you need. For example, it doesn't take much more fuel to boil eight potatoes than it does to do four, and the next day it requires less fuel to merely heat or fry them than actually to cook them. Things will cook faster if they are cut into small pieces: dice potatoes; cut a whole chicken into parts. Refrain from taking the lid off heating pots — this allows heat to escape, for which you pay by using more fuel. Cook two or three things in the same pot, thereby using one-half or one-third the amount of fuel that these foods would have taken if done on separate burners. Carrots, onions and potatoes do well in the same pot. Or you can add potatoes to the chicken pot when the chicken has just five minutes to go. Things cook no more rapidly at a fast boil than they do at a slow boil, so reduce your heat until the contents are just barely boiling.

Small is beautiful. The smaller the boat in which you can live aboard comfortably, the less the struggle to pay it off. Using smaller amounts of fuel enables you to choose a smaller boat, as you don't need extra footage to store fuel. Less money spent on fuel and footage means less time working to pay for it, and more time sailing off into the real world. That is why, in part, you bought your boat in the first place. "Think small, that's all."

Chapter 10:
Spend Less Time in the Galley

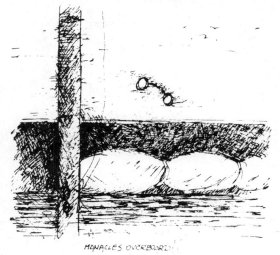

MANACLES OVERBOARD

The seventeenth-century galley slave was not happy with his lot. There was no end to the rowing, and boats being boats, the galleys were cramped, tempers flared and every now and then, all hell broke loose. Today's galley slave wears no manacles but some things don't change. There's no end to the meals, galleys are cramped, tempers flare and every now and then, all hell breaks loose.

The big difference between the two breeds of galley slaves is that the twentieth-century variety has some control over his or her lot, while those unfortunate others had none. And so, while on bad days we are still slaves, on good days we can be creative within certain limitations — which is all even the most fortunate in any lifestyle can ask.

We of the modern galley are free to call upon our wits and imagination to make life more palatable. Change those things in the galley that irritate and our time aboard will be more mellow.

There is no way out of the galley. But there are innumerable ways to spend less time there. I delight in whipping up in minutes what appears to be a why-you-must-have-slaved-over-a-hot-stove-all-day type meal. Cooking is fun, but only if you have time for other things too.

If some of the ideas mentioned below appear to be paltry

and of only slight time-saving value, you're quite right! But taken together, they chop whole hours off galley duty.

First of all, there are some tools that are real time-savers. The *French rocker knife* is a chopping knife that comes in various sizes, and costs anywhere from ten to twenty dollars, depending on size and quality. Once you acquire the knack of using it, you will be chopping mountains in minutes. Holding the handle in your right hand (if you're right-handed), the fingers of the left hand press firmly on the tip of the blade, while the right hand rocks the blade rapidly up and down, transforming a large onion into a pile of finely diced bits in less than a minute. It takes practice — you won't be fast at first. If you do a lot of chopping for salads and sauces, it's a skill worth learning.

A knive is an effective aid only when it is sharp. There should be a *knife sharpener* easily accessible (or mounted) and it should become habit to use it frequently.

Knives are the most frequently used utensil in a galley and should themselves be mounted so that they can be reached quickly without pawing through other items in a drawer or bin. Also, in a bin the edge is subject to damage from collision with other things and this can turn a once sharp and fast tool into an inefficient, blunted object that deserves all the names you can call it.

One last thing about knives: have a *good selection*. A bread knife does a very slow job of chopping vegetables; a paring knife does a slow job on a roast.

Water is used so often in meal preparation that the kind of *hand pump* that requires ten or more pumps to produce water should be discarded in favor of either a hand pump which produces water immediately, or a *foot pump*. A foot pump can be working on getting the water up to the sink while both hands are carrying on with other things. Sometimes, in order to use the hand pump you have to first relocate a pile of dishes that is blocking the handle, and that takes time. There is rarely any clutter in the way of a foot pump.

A *thermos* eliminates the time it takes to get the stove going and wait for the water to boil for coffee throughout the day. For a boat, it should be stainless steel. Stainless steel thermoses are expensive, but they last literally forever. There is the occasional dud that keeps water hot for only two or three hours, and these can be returned to the manufacturer and replaced free of charge.

An additional wide-mouthed thermos should be considered for Dutch oven cooking. The wide mouth facilitates cleaning. You can also make yogurt in the thermos, a process that is less trouble than using an electric yogurt maker. Just put the warm yogurt mixture in the thermos in the evening and you'll have fresh yogurt ready for breakfast.

A *whistling tea kettle* boils water more quickly than one that does not have a cover over the spout, for the same reason that a covered pot boils more quickly than an uncovered one.

If you make a lot of biscuits or quick breads, a *pastry blender* is the perfect tool for breaking the shortening into the flour. It does in seconds what would otherwise take several minutes. The pastry blender also chops up hard-boiled eggs in record time, for a faster egg salad sandwich.

I have dealt extensively with the *pressure cooker* else-where. Let me say that of all the things that can help you spend less time in the galley, the pressure cooker ranks number one, and number two is far behind. Anyone who wishes to reduce time spent in the galley should get one.

Cook's duties are not over when the cooking is done. *Dishes* can take as long as meal preparation. One way to cut down on the time it takes to wash dishes is to cut down on the dishes used. Paper plates are an obvious option. I hate paper plates — they use up a dwindling natural resource, they make garbage, and they incriminate me as a member of the disposable society. But I keep a stack of them to use when we have a crowd for dinner. It keeps me from feeling put upon, put out, and put down at having to do a huge pile of dishes after barely resting from preparing the meal.

Another way to cut down on *dishes* to wash is to serve meals that can be eaten with no plates and no utensils — the kind of meals that can be carried about. This is often appreciated by those on board — they don't have to miss the scenery while eating a more formal meal below.

For breakfast, a toasted western sandwich (a fried egg with ketchup between two pieces of toast) is a good one, or a toasted bacon and tomato sandwich, or hard-boiled eggs and a plate of bite-sized fruit, or cornbread and honey. For lunch, any kind of fritter is a good finger food, served with a plate of tomatoes sliced into wedges.

Corned beef fritters are delicious. Chop a medium onion very finely. Mix the onion into a 12 ounce tin of corned beef. With your fingers, roll the corned beef-onion mixture into balls of about an inch in diameter. Dip each ball into batter (1 cup of flour, 1 teaspoon baking powder, 1 well-beaten egg,

3/4 cup water or milk). Drop into a pot of hot oil until golden.

For supper you can serve chicken wings and legs with corn on the cob, spareribs, hamburgers or hot dogs. Instead of a salad which requires bowls and forks, serve a large plate of finger vegetables: radishes, green onions, chunks of cauliflower, and so on. And don't feel you have to spend time fancying up the radishes and carrots into radish roses and carrot curls. They look beautiful, fresh and wholesome just the way they are. Rinse, scrub them if necessary, and that's all.

A practice which cuts dishwashing time in half is to never dry dishes. Let them drip dry, and put them away later. If you have a double sink, they can drip dry in the half you are not using, and be out of the way, even out of sight, if you have a sink cover. If you must use counter space for the drip drying, it is often not a feasible practice as you may need the counter for other things. And some people don't like the clutter out in plain sight. If you're under way, or will be soon, you will have to stow the dishes anyway. The perfect arrangement for drip drying is to have your dishes and utensils stored in racks that drain back into the sink. The dishes can then go straight from the rinse water to the rack, and you don't have to bother with them again — simple, neat, and a huge time-saver. It is also more hygienic than rubbing each item with a tea towel that has been used for dear knows what, and hasn't been washed in who knows how long.

Dishes are easier and faster to wash if they are done immediately after the meal, before the food has had a chance to stick to the plates as if it were a kind of epoxy. But if the food does stick hard, or is burned on, don't waste your time scrubbing, scraping and cursing — drop the dishes into a bucket and let them soak. Water is the greatest solvent, and after a few hours of the water treatment, or overnight, dishes wipe clean in no time.

Don't automatically wash everything that was used in preparing the meal. For example, lids rarely need to be actually washed, just wiped dry. The frying pan shouldn't need washing if it is kept well oiled. After frying an egg, wipe the pan with a paper towel or dry cloth. That is all it should need. And in fact, the frying pan that is kept constantly oiled and not washed will have fewer problems with food sticking and burning.

Dishes will take less time if you avoid using tools that require a long time to wash. An egg beater takes about ten times longer to clean than a fork, and unless you make meringue daily, a fork will do just as well. (Professionals use two forks, one on top of the other, separated slightly with a finger.) And for whipping cream, pour eight ounces of whipping cream into a jar that would hold twice that amount and shake. This whips cream faster than an egg beater, and the jar is faster to clean than an egg beater. The egg poacher is another beast to clean. Either have soft-boiled eggs instead, or poach eggs in a small pot of water.

Try to avoid tools that take a long time to assemble, such as the meat grinder. It is usually enough to finely chop or grate the item. I keep a grinder on board for grinding conch for fritters, as nothing else is adequate for the job.

A habit we adopted on board years ago, and it's not a bad idea on land either, is to issue a mug to each person — they are then responsible for its whereabouts and its state of cleanliness. The mug is used by the same person for all beverages during the day. This way, if you have a crowd on board, people will not grab a fresh glass every time they want another drink, and keep you washing glasses all day.

With the following trick, you can reduce the number of spoons used for making coffee from several to just one: leave one spoon in the coffee jar, one in the sugar jar, one in the milk jar (if a powder is used) and keep a stirring spoon in a special spot. Everybody uses the stirring spoon, and it gets washed once a day.

Plan to have leftovers. It's marvelous not even to have to think about at least one meal a day. When preparing supper, make extra for lunch the next day. Then, come lunch time, all you have to do is heat it up. Or cook an extra potato so it can be fried in the morning. Or cook double the amount of squash, serve it in chunks the first night, and mashed the next. Even without refrigeration, food (with the exception of fish and fowl) will keep twenty-four hours. However, it should not be stored in aluminum pots, as some foods break down aluminum and then you ingest it, and there is such a thing as aluminum poisoning.

Some hints about *specific foods*: Don't peel potatoes, just scrub them. The skin is tasty and has many vitamins. And the potatoes will cook faster if cut into small pieces.

Don't peel tomatoes, apples, and so on. I make apple crisp with the apple skins on — they are noticeably there but are not unpleasant.

Recently, I was aghast to run across someone who peels

mushrooms; she must really not know what to do with her spare time!

When chopping celery, leave the stalks attached to the crown and chop all nine or ten stalks at the same time instead of one at a time.

Put a whole handful of green beans on the cutting board and cut all at once, instead of painstakingly one or two at a time.

Spinach and other greens can be washed quickly by immersing the entire bagful in a large basin of water and gently dunking several times. Sand and other debris will sink to the bottom.

Don't take the time to carve out the interior of a green pepper — use it seeds and all. Seeds are nutritious.

The shipboard chef sometimes sees himself as a creature chained to the galley and at those times his duties become drudgery. We all wear manacles of some sort. The trick is to learn how to loosen the wretched things and one fine day, slip them off and toss them overboard.

Chapter 11:
The "Perfect" Galley

GARBAGE DISPOSAL WITH A VIEW.

Having lost our 46' *Isla* on the reef (see Part I), and now the proud owners of the 29' *Mariposa*, a once-rotting derelict of the same design, we were, I suppose, in an enviable position. We'd had the chance to plan two galleys, try them out, and thus acquire the proper perspective from which to plan the perfect galley. (Saying "perfect" in relation to galleys is always accompanied by much eye rolling and little chuckles.)

The basics are easy — they are the guidelines for almost every aspect of our life on board, and, for that matter on shore. A galley should be safe, simple and aesthetically pleasing. And after our experience on the 29' tri, we had to add another: adequate space. To accommodate the size of our perfect galley, our perfect boat (another tri) will be thirty-five feet.

The galley must have standing head room. Hunching over is fine for a weekend, but wears thin when living aboard full time. We know a fellow who cruised and hunched for years. It didn't bother him, but it would drive us whacky. We expanded the five-foot four-inch galley headroom on *Mariposa* to six feet two inches by lowering the floorboards and adding a rounded hatch over the galley area.

The galley should be located immediately forward of the steering station so that the person on watch has easy access to snacks. This location also places the galley centrally, where motion is minimal. If located further forward, galleys become roller coasters — great for sea stories later but not great for meals (or the stomach) at the time.

The passage through the galley should be wide enough for two people to pass comfortably. On the *Mariposa*, either the cook has to move right out of the galley, or the two people must gyrate sideways so that their bodies mesh together during the slide past. Cozy, you say? Just try it.

The galley and table must be on the same side as the steering station so that neither the galley nor table lights impair the helmsman's night vision.

My husband and I often like to work on a meal together. For this reason, we would avoid the narrow U galley that many cruisers prefer, because a lurching body can be wedged into it. Our perfect gally will be a wide U, which is preferable to the L-shaped because it gives more counter space, and because the forward end of the U serves as a spot from which things can be easily passed to and from the table.

The chart table on the starboard side is glorious counter space most of the time. Beneath the chart table are the cooler and garbage bin, parts of the galley that are not used frequently enough to become a bother when the chart table is in constant use.

A refrigeration system would complicate our life afloat. It breaks down, and parts are difficult to get in out-of-the-way places. It's expensive — one of us would have to work to pay for the thing (and working is not sailing). Generators are noisy and smelly and may themselves break down, and pilot flames are a hazard. No, thank you! But it is a delight occasionally to have ice. The answer is a well-insulated hull-shaped cooler, top-opening to keep the cold in, and built flush with the counter so as not to break up the space. The interior should be stainless steel or epoxy (polyester taints food).

A large garbage bin that encloses the smell, sight and mess when the bag breaks is important. There's nothing worse than trying to cook with the aroma of sour milk, moldy oranges and used tobacco wafting through the air. The bin should be removable so that the mess can be sluiced out by taking the whole bin into the cockpit.

I like a small (10 x 14-inch) sink because I hate to give up counter space. A sink cover helps provide extra space. But inevitably, because you need the sink while you use the counter, or because you're tired of cleaning out the food bits that fall into the crack, the sink remains a hole in the counter. The bigger the sink, the bigger the hole.

Something I've always wanted is a small opening port in the hull over the sink through which I could jettison all biodegradable garbage. When we cruise at sea, our only saved garbage is bottles and plastic. This would keep the counter uncluttered, and save steps to the cockpit.

A four-inch-deep drawer with at least five divisions is essential for utensils. To have to hunt for a spoon among a tangle of eggbeaters, forks and can openers causes this lady to erupt like Vesuvius — with not so much as one preliminary rumble. And pawing through a pile of disorganized items actually causes panic when the boat is heaving in a sloppy sea, it's dark, the flashlight won't work, and you may be needed any minute for a sail change. An uncluttered galley makes for an uncluttered mind. And that's a good way to sail.

A two-burner stove with no ovens has always been adequate for us, even when we were doing chartering with *Isla*. The use of usually two and sometimes three pressure cookers made this possible. Kerosene is the only fuel we would consider. It is cheap, produces a hot flame and is available in far-flung places. The ignition temperature is low, and fumes are not heavier than air, so they do not sink into the bilge to wait for a stray spark.

This "perfect" galley will also have a gravity-fed tank for fresh water and a foot pump for sea water. So much sea water is used on a cruising boat that fetching it in a bucket becomes tiresome after a while and in fact is downright dangerous when you're surging along at six knots or more. The gravity feed for fresh water, unlike the pressure system, is simple, it never breaks down, and it makes no noise.

My basic cooking ingredients will be kept in square glass jars (ten-ounce Nescafé jars are perfect) behind the counter and held in place by a fiddle. Having them all in sight keeps the culinary creativity flowing. They make the galley look interesting too, with their varied contents: green mung beans, red kidney beans, brown sugar, honey, flour and so on. And one jar will be kept full of baking soda, *brightly* marked, ready to throw on a flash fire.

Gary and I both like the warmth and harmony that natural wood radiates, so there will be a lot of it in the new galley.

But Gary has always had a thing about stainless steel counters. His reasons are good: they are safe, easy to clean, and easy to maintain. "Are you sure you don't want stainless steel counters?" he asked, broaching the old subject, thinking perhaps I'd learned something from the always-stained painted surfaces on *Mariposa* and from the arborite that lifted on *Isla*.

"No", I said, immovable. "I don't want to feel that I'm working in a restaurant. Stainless steel is cold and uninspiring. My boat is my home. I want the counters to be of wood, coated with clear urethane."

Gary gave in. We'd had a urethaned wood counter on *Isla* after the arborite lifted, and it added a beautiful warm glow to the galley. It was easy to clean, and stains and dents were never eyesores, they just seemed to add character. To make this somewhat flammable surface safe, we designed a two-inch deep well out of stainless steel into which the stove fit. This would contain a fire caused by fuel leaks. The stove should also be set back at least ten inches from the edge of the counter to prevent accidental turning of the knobs and to keep clothes, flesh and hair as far away as possible from the flame.

Our new perfect boat is still in the planning stages and we're quite happy with it there. We can't find a thing wrong with it, and other than the occasional polishing of details it's virtually maintenance-free.

Other boaters, too, indulge in a little polishing of their dream boats and it's interesting to compare what they consider to be priorities. Some veteran cruisers list their ideas here.

Barbara Winter, live-aboard for five years with husband and nine children (yes, I said nine!): good ventilation; ability to see the horizon; oven for baking bread; stove close to table; no refrigeration; pressure cookers; seed sprouter; thermos; deep, double sinks.

Don McGregor, live-aboard for ten years: deep, double sinks; gravity-fed water (preferably rain-fed from the cabin top); foot pump for sea water; U or L galley to give as much counter space as possible; nesting pots; a big Dutch oven and/or one or two pressure cookers and/or a well-insulated folding oven; two-burner kerosene stove. And, he adds jokingly, a good woman to share it all with.

Janet Groene, live-aboard for many years and author of the very complete *The Galley Book:* safety; pressure cooker to save time, fuel and reduce heat in cabin; large, deep sinks; stove covers, slide out shelves, hinge-up shelves, and so on, for extra counter space; a good stove — Janet lived aboard for ten years with a two-burner kerosene and loved it. She rates alcohol "somewhere down next to building a beach fire with wet moss."

Fiona McCall, whose accounts of cruising aboard a twenty-one-foot sailboat have appeared in the *Toronto Sun* and *Canadian Yachting* magazine: high fiddles; counter space on both sides of the sink; dish rack that is permanent storage and allows wet dishes to drain into the sink; strong lock latches on doors. An oven, she says, is not essential but is nice to provide variety of flavor.

Beth Holland, live-aboard for five years: two foot pumps, one salt, one fresh; good lighting (an Alladin kerosene mantle); good ventilation (overhead hatch); galley open to the salon to allow cook to take part in the conversation; large kerosene stove with oven. She wants to replace her miniature sink, which is "more of a nuisance than anything," with large, deep, double sinks.

Margaret Roth of *Whisper*: a U-shaped galley with a strap that she can wedge herself into; a galley open to the salon; a gimballed kerosene stove placed low. She uses a diesel stove in colder climates.

Faye Solovtzoff, live-aboard cook on a large charter vessel for several years: extractor fan or good cross ventilation; reliable lighting that gives off a minimum of heat; ability to reach tools and appliances without effort; knife rack, to avoid injury and to preserve sharp edges. And she adds, "As we sailed over the horizon, I'd pray fervently for cheerful company, enthusiastic appetites, and a pre-dinner rum."

Chapter 12:
Stock Your Boat in Spring

Springtime is sailing time. The dreams spawned during winter's hibernation come to life. With fulfillment in sight, you and your boat throb with new vitality. But vaguely you recall the frustrations of other years: how, with all the other demands on your free time, the summer's sailing had to be squeezed into a few too-short weekends; or how the entire season seemed relegated to a few too-short evenings. Not enough time, you scream silently.

This year, instead of shaking a futile fist at Time, get in tune with it. There are numerous little tricks you can employ that will enable you to stretch your time on the water. One is to become a missing person — this will free you of family responsibilities. Another is to become a drunk — this will get you fired, unless you have the misfortune of working for a company that rehabilitates such people.

The one trick I want to elaborate on is stocking your boat for the entire season in the early spring, even before she goes in the water. This will add hours of extra sailing time. In addition, your mind will be left uncluttered for more pleasurable pursuits, like planning how to convert that piece of aluminum tubing into a spinnaker pole. You won't have to keep muttering mindlessly to yourself, "I must remember the relish and the coffee," and the thousand other things. Being stocked for the entire season will also add to your spontaneity — you will be able to depart anytime, and not have to stop to pick up anything. This will eliminate hours of fuming in lineups at grocery stores. If you have a large, ballasted keelboat, you will not be concerned with either the bulk or weight of your foods. But if your boat is a monohull on the small side, you may prefer to stock dried or powdered products, which occupy far less space than their tinned equivalents. And if your boat is a multihull, on which weight above the water line is a consideration, you should select dried foods for this reason. On multihulls less than thirty-two feet, large quantities of heavy items (water, fruit juices, soft drinks, cases of beans) should be stored below the water line, preferably in the bilge.

You will have to choose foods that do not require refrigeration and which will not deteriorate or melt (as chocolate bars do when temperatures soar inside the closed boat). And you will want to choose foods that are not elaborately packaged so that your evenings and weekends are not spent disposing of mounds of trash. Anything that comes in porous containers should be repackaged to keep out moisture and bugs. Tupperware and Frig-O-Seal (less expensive and, from my experience, just as good — available in almost all grocery stores) are excellent for this. For larger quantities, you can often buy two or three-gallon airtight containers from bakeries.

Here are some ideas for foods that you can stock for the entire sailing seasor..

Some salamis keep for years, but do check the label to be sure it doesn't say "keep refrigerated." We have kept salami on board for six months — the outside wrapper turned green and fuzzy, but the inside was fresh and good. Cheese will keep for months if completely submerged in cooking oil in an airtight container. But the cheese must be uncontaminated at the time of purchase, that is, taken from an uncut round of cheese. If your boat is well-ventilated (and cool), you can buy and preserve a two-month supply of eggs by smearing them with vaseline — but the eggs must be fresh and never refrigerated. If the boat is hot when closed up, try powdered eggs, which are fine for baking and making scrambled eggs.

Dried fruits and vegetables are now common. Dried apples, apricots, and pineapples are tasty snacks, and they make a superb breakfast when set to soak the night before and served with a muffin. Dried carrots, green peppers, onions and other vegetables reconstitute and cook in ten minutes or so and are great for adding to one-pot meals.

Many a one-pot meal depends on hamburger, which is easily canned. The one-pint Mason jars hold about 3/4 pound of fried hamburger — enough for spaghetti sauce for three or four people. Chunks of beef (always the cheap cut because the canning process makes even the toughest meat tender) and pork (for sweet and sour pork one night, perhaps) can be canned, too.

There are tinned brown breads (sweet), which are delicious for snacking or for lunches. Delicatessens sell tinned soda bisuits, while there are also many types of tinned biscuits, sweet and otherwise. Grocery stores sell muffin mixes, and natural foods stores sell a master mix that makes everything (pancakes, breads) just by adding different amounts of water or milk. Of course, you can make all of these things from scratch, but when your time aboard is limited, dealing with basics may detract from your enjoyment.

A fairly new item on the market is dried salad, available from natural foods stores. It consists of dried bulgur or rice and dried vegetables. You add oil and water and let it sit for an hour. The result is delicious and chewy. The salad can be made crunchier by adding dried onions at the last minute, or a handful of chopped almonds.

If there are usually only two people on board and you expect to be sailing every other weekend and one evening a week during a four-month period, you should plan for sixteen breakfasts, sixteen lunches, thirty-two suppers and thirty-two snacks (if you snack). You might stock the following:

tinned brown bread/10
tinned soda biscuits/3, 1 pound each
tinned sweet biscuits/3, 1 pound each
master mix/6 pounds
cheese/6 pounds
salami/4 pounds
tinned tuna/10
tinned ham/3
tinned bacon/4
powdered eggs/6 dozen
parmesan cheese/1 large
canned hamburger (or tinned equivalent)/8
canned beef (or tinned equivalent)/8
canned pork (or tinned equivalent)/8

tinned pork and beans/6
spaghetti/3 pounds   noodles/3 pounds
lentils/2 pounds
tinned potatoes/10
tinned tomato paste/10
tinned corn/8
tinned green beans/8
tinned peas/8
tinned mushrooms/8
dried fruit/4 pounds
dried vegetables/3 pounds
dried salad/20 packages
almonds and walnuts/3 pounds
pickles and olives/10 small jars
tinned butter or margarine/3 pounds, in small lots
soups (dried or tinned)/10
peanut butter/2 pound jars
popping corn/1 pound
granola bars/5 boxes
raisins/3 pounds
sugar/3 pounds
tea, coffee, hot chocolate, dried individual-serving soups
powdered milk/10 quarts
vegetable oil/32 ounces
vinegar/32 ounces
bouillon cubes/12 each of beef and chicken
salt, pepper, garlic powder and soy sauce
tinned fruit juices/24, 16 ounces each
beer and rum/enough

The only hitch in all this is ice. It *is* nice to have cold drinks on hot days. Although we sailed for years without ice and did come to enjoy room temperature drinks, it's not likely that everyone will want to try this, and I'm not sure I'd want to do it again. If the next time you're speeding down to the boat, your only stop is for ice, you've come a long way.

Be sure your galley is also well-stocked with equipment. Don't wait half the summer to get a paring knife or a pressure cooker. Stockpile all the galley gear during the winter, then on launching day get it all stowed. For food, make your list in March, buy the stuff in April, and stow it in May. From here on in it's smooth sailing.

You will then feel at the outset of the season that you and your boat are ready to take off at a moment's notice (except, of course, for repairing the engine, the leak, the snatch block, the clew out-haul .... It will be as though you've spent the whole summer sailing instead of just going out for a sail every now and then between bouts of harbor fever.

Chapter 13:
Stocking the Multihull

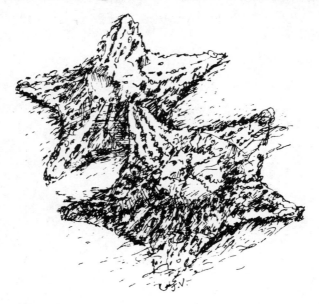

To me, there are two basic steps to stocking the multihull. If you embark on step one, you're committed to following with step two. 1) Buy dried foods primarily. 2) Learn how to cook them.

The main consideration behind these points is weight, which can be critical on a multihull. The consequence of overloading is reduced speed, which in heavy seas and high winds means reduced safety; the vessel will not run away quickly from a curling sea; and it will be more sluggish when turning out of a broaching situation. The importance of weight is much more critical on a multihull than a monohull. While a forty-foot unloaded multihull may weigh only four tons, a forty-foot monohull may weigh fourteen tons, often more. Thus a thousand pounds of food (enough for a family of four for approximately six months) adds about twelve per cent more weight to the multihull, which is considerable, while it only adds about two per cent more weight to the monohull, which is negligible.

On the average, dried foods have about eighty per cent of their weight removed. Therefore, a sixteen-ounce tin of beans will serve two meals, while a sixteen-ounce bag of dried beans will serve ten meals. And each occupies about the same amount of space. This means that instead of carrying one thousand pounds of tinned foods, you need carry only two hundred pounds of dried foods, adding only two per cent more weight to the forty-foot multihull. For the small multihull, this means that instead of trying to find a hundred square feet of bilge in which to store the food, you need only find twenty square feet.

So dried foods are the ideal choice for the multihull in terms of weight. But are they nutritious? After all, safety at sea involves good nutrition — a well-maintained body, like a well-maintained boat, is more seaworthy than one that is not.

Dried foods provide excellent nutrition for shipboard meals. Many of the dried foods you choose will be beans, seeds and nuts. Because they all contain the necessary ingredients to start new life, when made to sprout they produce great quantities of vitamins, minerals and enzymes. They also contain a lot of protein, some of them as much as meat.

Dried fruits and vegetables, especially if they are sun-dried, retain more minerals and vitamins than their tinned equivalents. Dried meats (jerky and sausage) lose none of their food value. Use powdered milk — skim milk is available in powdered form only in the United States and Canada, but you can buy powdered whole milk in the Bahamas and other countries.

Dried foods are often better for you than their tinned counterparts for another reason. They are not contaminated by the numerous additives injected into almost all canned goods, such as salt, sugar, BHA, BHT, sodium erythrobate, sodium nitrite (carcinogenic) and many, many others.

On a boat, dried foods have the further advantage of lasting literally forever if properly stored. Tinned goods will not — some have a shelf life of less than a year. Carrots seem to be particularly short-lived. On several boats I've seen puffy tins of carrots that had been stowed less than ten months. Tins are also prone to rusting, especially in salt water, which will decrease their shelf life. And even in a tin that is not rusted, you have the danger of botulism — this is something you never have to worry about with dried foods.

Dried foods must be kept in airtight containers to keep out all moisture and bugs. Plastic gallon jars are available at some delicatessen stores, and plastic five-gallon pails are available at some bakeries, restaurants and natural foods stores. The best pails are those with lids that must be pried off with a screwdriver. There are some sturdy five-gallon olive jugs available at some restaurants that serve Greek food. To discourage bugs from entering if you should get pails that aren't quite airtight, throw in a few bay leaves. But if you want to be absolutely sure of keeping out bugs and of even killing any bugs or eggs that may already be in the food, try dry ice. It has been used by long-distance sailors for years. The ice sublimates into carbon dioxide, which kills the bugs. A piece of about 1½ inches in diameter is enough for a six-gallon container. If the chunk is too big, the container will explode. This can be avoided by lifting up the edge of the lid every now and then as the sublimation takes place.

Cost is another area where dried foods win out. A dollar will buy about six meals of tinned peas and about eighteen meals of dried peas. Buying in bulk also saves money, and although regular grocery stores do not allow bulk purchases, natural foods stores will give discounts if you buy in bulk — this usually means five or ten pound lots. Some stores give a further discount if you buy over a hundred dollars worth of goods. The store I deal with gives me a thirty per cent discount for orders over a hundred dollars. Although food is in general more expensive at natural foods stores, bulk buying and large orders can bring the cost somewhat below regular grocery store prices.

Greater variety is yet another plus in stocking dried foods. There are many dried foods that are not available in tinned form, and which add variety, flavor and nutrition to the diet. Soy beans, for instance, are as high in protein as meat, and make excellent "meat" patties. There are also pinto beans, black beans, navy beans and lentils. Dried green peppers are great in a lot of dishes and add vitamin D and chlorophyl to the diet. Plain wheat holds great potential for breakfast cereals and sprouts.

More variety can be achieved by combining two or more beans or grains in one dish, often resulting in a more complete protein and a more nutritious dish. (Read *Diet For a Small Planet* by Frances Moore Lappé for a complete discussion of this idea.) And by simply adjusting the quantity of water you add, you can vary the consistency of dried foods to make soup, vegetables, or "meat" loaf.

Packaged breakfast cereals occupy a lot of space, and on a small multihull there just isn't room for them. (It *is* a good idea to have one box of bran well wrapped in plastic for use as a laxative.) The whole-grain dry cereals — Vita-B, Red River (available only in Canada), rolled oats — offer excellent nutrition, contain no chemicals, are easy to use and take up about 1/10 the space that packaged cereals do. Millet (available in natural foods stores) is a pleasant change, and contains three times the protein of oats. If prepared the night before (or even an hour before) and then reheated with perhaps a little extra water to make the consistency exactly right, these whole grain cereals will have a fuller flavor and creamier texture.

If you sail to cultures that are more basic than technology-oriented North America, I think that the use of basic foodstuffs can help to lessen the barriers between you and local peoples.

The traveler who has used and understands his own basic foods is more on an equal footing with these people. The culture gap between a technology-oriented society and one that is not is potentially great. Technology is responsible for this gap and it is therefore up to the one who comes from technology to attempt to close the gap. People from a more basic culture can relate better to someone who uses, for instance, flour and dried beans to make a meal instead of opening two or three tins. It's like motoring through Mexico: you get to know the people better if you are driving a battered-up half ton rather than a gleaming airstream. The half ton is within their grasp — they use and understand them. Traveling in an airstream, or cooking with a can opener, often puts a barrier between people. And not just because the local people cannot understand technology. It is more because the can opener people are not accustomed to dealing with basics, and this perspective (or lack of perspective) makes them unable to relate to what they see. As much as possible, extraneous obstacles should be cancelled out. I think that using dried foods and other basic foods is a way of removing one of the obstacles.

A final advantage to stocking dried foods is that it satisfies the desire to be self-sufficient, which is probably the basic drive that motivates most men and women who yearn to sail in a small boat. Cooking on board can also add immeasurably to the boating experience, as long as you don't feel trapped by it. The ease of using dried foods will allow you the time for other things, like reading Farley Mowat's *The Boat Who Wouldn't Float*, or oiling the teak. But primarily, the value of dried foods is in the nutrition and variety they provide, and in their relatively light weight, which adapts so well to the purposes of the multihull sailor.

Chapter 14:
Rotate Cooks: Everyone Wins

"HEY, WHO'S STEERING THIS BOAT, ANYWAY?"

Why do some women love the sea, and others hate it? Why is it that some women jump at the chance to go sailing and others are always looking for an excuse not to? And how on earth does it happen that the boat (the goddamn boat, to use many a woman's choice of words) wedges itself between two people, like a demanding mistress, and pushes them apart?

It is easy to say that there are as many reasons as there are couples, but this makes finding a solution difficult. If there were some general pattern to the woman's growing disaffection (many women start out neutral or only vaguely opposed), then a general solution might be proposed.

In fact, this problem — which probably afflicts seventy-five per cent of all boaters at one time or another — does follow a pattern and stems from one basic cause: fear. Fear of doing the wrong thing, fear of being yelled at, fear of drowning, fear of being bored. And as if that's not enough, there's the fear of losing the man she loves if she doesn't learn to love the boat she fears. All this certainly gives her mixed emotions about the g.d. boat.

Strangely enough, these fears very often revolve around the galley and how much time the woman is expected to spend (or insists on spending) there. But, when you think about it, it makes sense. For it is not in the galley that she will learn how to hoist the main, backwind the jib, reverse the engine, be surefooted, or acquire an interest in marine life, navigation and boat maintenance. However, it is the learning of these things that will eradicate her fear and turn her into a willing and effective deckhand eager to explore that cove over the horizon.

As a woman whose first major boating experience (a four-month cruise on the Pacific) was aboard a vessel where galley duty was shared equally among the four crew, I speak as a person who loves the sea. But I might never have come to love it if most of my time on board had been predetermined by sex. I also speak as a sailor, which I might never have become had my major duties been below deck.

It was the captain's idea that galley duty be rotated, and that each person do full galley chores for an entire day. For the four individuals, that meant each had to cook one day in four. That way all the galley work did not fall on the one woman aboard: me. The men all said they'd pitch in, but the captain wisely suspected there might be a large gap between talk and reality. Hence, he proposed *regulated* pitching in. We all supported his idea. Tradition dies hard, though, and I felt vaguely guilty. But not for long.

The four of us — Don McGregor, his then thirteen-year-old son Lew, my husband Gary and I — kept up this cook-for-one-day-in-four routine for three months, aboard Don's 42' trimaran *La Paz*. Eighteen for dinner or just the four of us, at anchor or riding out a gale at sea, the routine never varied.

Besides giving me the opportunity to learn to sail and giving the men a chance to learn to cook, this system had other unexpected fringe benefits. Culinary creations became artistic and adventurous. Meals became a performance of sorts and extra touches were always noticed and applauded. There was also a noticeable upward swing in morale aboard, because duty was no longer the drudgery that everyday routine makes it. And because of the equal responsibility basis of the system, no one could play martyr, no one could shirk.

One thing we noticed when living on board for even a week is that there are two main activities to shipboard life: navigation, and eating (and all that that entails). They occupy close-to-equal amounts of time. The one ensures the safety of all, the other the well-being. What a lot of you miss if you're involved in only one or the other!

An unexpected benefit of regulated galley duty relates to

the joy of cooking, which comes, I think, from the fact that it is an active form of giving of yourself to others. In this age of individualism, it is sometimes hard to find an acceptable way of giving, sometimes hard to find a recipient. This problem is easily solved by the system of preordained days of cooking established on *La Paz*.

Lew summed it up one day when he exclaimed, "This eating business is getting to be great fun!"

As a woman freed from slaving in the galley, I expressed the other side of the coin. "This sailing's the life!"

PART III
Galley Fare

Chapter 1:
Bread

When you are setting out for a two-week trip on the boat, you don't want to be dependent on grocery stores and have to pull into port because you've run out of bread, or because it's all turning green.

There are two tricks you can use when you're stocking the boat that will extend the life of bread. One is to buy bakery bread and ask the baker to *double bake* it for you. This puts a tough crust on the loaf, which protects it from the damp atmosphere of the boat. The bread will then keep fresh for up to ten days.

The other trick is to convert your bread, preferably fresh from a bakery or your own oven, into *rusks* sometime before you leave port. Cut a loaf into thick slices. Place the slices on racks or trays in a warm oven until browned and crisped. Store in an airtight container. What this rebaking does to the bread is to remove the moisture on which mold would grow. Rusks will keep for months. They are a great base for a sloppy Joe, or creamed salmon.

That gives you three bread options; start with fresh, switch to double-baked, finish up with rusks.

For variety, or to impress yourself with how independent of shore you've become, or because freshly baked things smell and taste so good, you may want to bake your own.

Yeast Bread

Living aboard *Mariposa* this past year with a baby, I never seemed to find the time to make this delicious bread, but Gary made it about once a week. He doesn't use a recipe any more and it's a little different each time he makes it, but this is what he started off with. The quantities make 1 loaf in a pressure cooker on top of the stove. Double the quantities for 2 loaves in an oven.

Into a large warm bowl (let hot water stand in it for a minute) put ½ cup lukewarm water, 1 teaspoon honey (sugar will do) and 2 tablespoons yeast (or 2 packets of Fleishman's yeast). Mix, and let stand for 10 minutes. If it is a cool day, cover with a towel to keep the water warm (yeast will not multiply in cold water).

Stir, making sure the yeast is well dissolved. Stir into the mixture

1 **cup lukewarm water**
¼ **cup honey (sugar will do, but the flavor will be more bland)**
2 **teaspoons salt**
¼ **cup vegetable oil (melted shortening will do)**

Stir in, 1 cup at a time, and beat until smooth

4 **cups flour, any combination (usually half white, half whole-wheat, but 3 cups white and 1 cup whole-wheat is very good too).**

Mix until the ball of dough is a smooth, cohesive mass. Sprinkle a board and the dough with flour and knead for several minutes, until the dough is elastic. Put the dough back into the bowl, smear with oil or shortening, cover with a towel and let rise in a warm, draft free place until double in size, about 2 hours. Punch down. Pat into a round shape. Place in a pressure cooker that has been well-greased and sprinkled with cornmeal or Cream of Wheat on the bottom and sides (to prevent burning). Cover with the lid from which you have removed the rubber sealing ring and again let rise in a warm spot until double in size. Bake over low heat with 1 flame tamer for 20 minutes and then over high heat for 5 minutes to form a crust. Flip to brown the top.

Saltwater Bread

Ocean sailors have been using this recipe, or ones similar to it, for years. It boasts two remarkable features which make it ideal for boaters at sea. It requires no fresh water, and calls for no kneading. The flours suggested are whole-grain ones, which do not have a high gluten content. They are therefore not greatly improved by the process of kneading, the purpose of which is to "develop" the gluten so that it will hold more air bubbles, which make it rise higher. We have used this recipe many times and find it delicious.

Mix together and let work for 5 minutes: 1½ cups lukewarm sea water, 2 tablespoons yeast and 1 tablespoon honey. Add 4 cups flour (any combination of whole-wheat, oat, rye) and mix thoroughly with a big spoon that can press the last bits of flour into the dough. Pat into a round shape. Let rise in a warm place until double in size, about 1½ hours in a pressure cooker that has been thickly greased and liberally sprinkled with cornmeal or Cream of Wheat on the bottom and up the sides. Bake over low flame with a flame tamer for 15 minutes, then over high flame for 15 minutes to form a crust. Flip the loaf and bake the other side in a similar fashion.

The warm spot you use for allowing the dough to rise can be on the engine block if the engine is or has recently been running, in a sheltered place in the sun with a black cloth over it, in a pan of hot water with a blanket over everything, or on the stove, which can be turned on for 30 seconds or so every time the pot cools down.

Yeast Rolls

Shape the dough from any bread or roll recipe into balls of about 1½ inches in diameter and place about ¾ inch apart on a thickly-greased, heavy-gauge frying pan. Let rise in a warm spot with the lid on until double in size. Keep the lid on and "bake" over medium heat with one flame tamer for about 10 minutes. Flip to brown the other side. For variety, mix into the dough some coconut, bacon bits, chopped dried fruit, cocoa and a bit of sugar, or anything that strikes your fancy.

Biscuits

These biscuits were the mainstay of our existence on a recent four-month cruise. We never got tired of them. They're easy to make, good to eat cold (but better hot), and keep for a long time (if they get the chance) without going moldy.

3	**cups flour**
4	**teaspoons baking powder**
½	**teaspoon salt**
¼	**cup sugar**
1	**cup shortening (or half margarine or butter)**
¾	**cup currants**
1	**egg, beaten with enough milk to make up ½ cup**

Mix thoroughly the flour, baking powder, salt and sugar. Cut in the shortening and margarine with a pastry blender until crumbly. Add currants. Stir in egg and milk. Roll out to ¼ inch thick. Cut in rounds for 2 pans full. If you want to do them all at once and spend less time at the stove, roll the dough into 1 big circle, like a pie crust. The diameter should be a bit smaller than the diameter of the frying pan, which should be a thick-bottomed one. Lay the circle of dough into the frying pan and cut into 4 or 6 wedges to facilitate turning. Fry over a medium heat with 1 flame tamer for 5 minutes each side, or until nicely browned. Cut into pie-shaped wedges and serve on a napkin, with coffee. No dishes or utensils to wash, which saves you time and water.

Corn Bread (Johnny Cake)

I awoke in the aft cabin to a gentle but persistent jerky motion. The swell rolling into harbor was causing *Isla* to strain forward on her dock lines every few seconds, and then to fall back resignedly. She seemed to be saying, "Come on you guys, let's get up and go!" So I got up.

It was a cool October morning and as I stepped through the companionway into the wheelhouse, I snuggled deeper into my heaviest wool sweater. The air was wet, filled with the dank droplets of a heavy mist. A splash off to port caught my ear and I stepped into the cockpit to investigate — a female mallard and her little ones. But wasn't this the wrong time of year to be raising a family in Lake Ontario? Perhaps mama mallard knew something I didn't, but already I could almost feel the ice extending its long fingers across the harbor. It was time for boats and birds to flee. We were ready. But was she, I worried.

Then, because we had guests aboard who would soon be wandering into the main salon, I gave breakfast a moment's attention. What came to mind was *Johnny Cake*. Its hot, steaming sweetness would take the chill out of this sunless morning. I set the large pressure cooker-canner, with a rack on the bottom, on a burner to preheat. (Because I use this pot mostly as an oven and only rarely for canning, I keep it stored without the rubber ring so that I don't have to remove the ring every time I want an oven.) I reached for the ingredients and started mixing. Five minutes later the batter was in the pan in the pressure cooker and I sat down with a cup of coffee. Half an hour later it was sitting in all its golden glory on the table when the first sleepy heads emerged. Said one lady, eyeing it hungrily, "Oh you shouldn't have gone to all that trouble." In reality, *Johnny Cake* is less trouble than bacon and eggs.

¾ **cup butter (or half butter, half shortening)**
1 **cup brown sugar**
3 **eggs, well beaten**
1¼ **cups milk**
1 **cup cornmeal**
2 **cups white flour (if you want to squeeze in a little extra food value you use 1½ cups white flour, and ½ cup whole-wheat or soy flour)**
3 **teaspoons baking powder**

Mix butter and sugar until creamy. Add eggs. Mix together the dry ingredients, and add alternately with milk. For variety, add 1/3 cup Brazil nuts or almonds, chopped. Don't keep stirring after all the ingredients have been mixed in. Pour into a greased pan and bake at 350°F for 30 minutes or until a knife inserted comes out clean. Slice and serve with butter and honey, or maple syrup. If some is left over, it is good the next morning toasted or fried.
In terms of nutrition, this is a complete breakfast. There is always greater nutritive value with a combination of grains. In this case there is wheat and corn. The corn meal supplies

vitamin A, of which the wheat has none, and roughage, which white flour totally lacks. The milk and eggs provide plenty of protein. People rave over *Johnny Cake*. They consider it special and something of a novelty. And they always find it irresistible.

Banana Bread

Banana Bread, like *Johnny Cake*, is a good, nutritious way to start a cool morning. It can also be served as a dessert, plain or with icing.

One year, we prudently (or so it seemed at the time) bought an entire stalk of bananas before departing Panama for Key West, Florida. Each day we felt them. Not ripe yet. Nope, not today. Then, one day there were a couple yellow enough and soft enough to eat — the next day, they were all ripe. Hot damn! What do you do with *forty* ripe bananas? To discard any was unthinkable. It was our duty, as we saw it, to somehow eat them all. You name it, we had it: banana fluff; banana stew; and a daily favorite for about a week was *Banana Bread*:

1	cup mushy bananas (usually 2 bananas)
¼	cup shortening or butter
¾	cup brown sugar
2	eggs
½	cup sour milk (add 2 teaspoons lemon juice or vinegar to a cup before filling it to the ½ mark with milk)
2	cups flour (half whole-wheat)
2	teaspoons baking powder
½	teaspoon baking soda
1	teaspoon salt
1	teaspoon lemon rind, grated (not essential but does add extra zing to the flavor)
½	cup chopped walnuts or almonds (almonds are superior in protein)

Mix together flour, baking powder, soda and salt. Mix the shortening and sugar until smooth, and add the eggs and bananas. Mix well. Add to this alternatively the milk and flour mixture. Mix well. Pour into a greased pan and bake at 350°F for 50 minutes. Let cool for ½ hour. Lather with butter, and eat while still warm. This can be made on top of the stove in a straight-sided frying pan or thick-bottomed pot, by using low heat and a flame tamer, and flipping to brown the top.

Dumplings

While dumplings are not bread, they are an excellent bread substitute that does not occur to most people when they run out of bread. Dumplings have all the same ingredients as bread, it is just the method of cooking that is different. They are a valuable addition to the boater's repertoire because they take only ten minutes and don't dirty an extra pot.

Mariposa was on a beam reach as we sailed into the anchorage at Staniel Cay in the Bahamas, looking around eagerly for boats we knew. The last few weeks had been pleasantly spent in secluded spots farther up island and we were looking forward to swapping sea stories with friends. To our delight the 56' trimaran *Tao* was at the dock. Dave Matthews, the skipper, had spent years building her in Frenchman's Bay (near Toronto, Canada). Since launching in 1975, she has payed her way by chartering out of Toronto Islands in the summer, and through the Caribbean islands in winter.

We anchored in the three-knot current and Gary rowed over while I fed the baby. I had a feeling he might come back with some food for supper — *Tao* sometimes had grouper left over from a dive — so I didn't go ahead with ours. And I was right, except his catch was not fare from the sea, it was fare from a freezer on the fritz — ten pounds of eye of round! Sue, first mate and hostess-cook, was having to discard it.

One of the reasons we don't have refrigeration on *Mariposa* is to avoid a hassle like this when it breaks down. However, this was one breakdown that didn't bother us a bit. We had sumptuous steak that night, and I popped the rest into the pressure cooker for 15 minutes at 15 pounds pressure to preserve it until morning. Dave, Sue, and crew Kenny came over for lunch the next day and I made a big pot of eye of round dumplings. Sue never makes dumplings, so it was something of an event for them. And it must have been good, for they each had three helpings.

Into a 6-quart pot place:

2   pounds eye of round, cut into bite-sized chunks and well cooked, either fried or pressure-cooked — fried

improves the flavor, but mine was pressure-cooked to halt possible bacterial growth

3   stalks celery, chopped
3   large carrots, diced or thinly sliced
3   large onions, chopped and sauteed
1   tomato, mashed
3   beef bouillon cubes
1   teaspoon salt
3   garlic cloves, crushed
1   teaspoon chili powder
1   teaspoon vinegar
1   teaspoon soy sauce
3   tablespoons flour dissolved in 1 cup water

Add water (or stock) to 2 inches above all the ingredients. Stir and heat until the gravy thickens. It should be on the thin side. Bring the stew to a boil and meanwhile prepare the dumplings:

2   cups flour (a nice combination is half white, half oat or half white, half whole-wheat)
½   teaspoon salt
4   teaspoons baking powder
1   heaping tablespoon Parmesan cheese (not essential — I add it purely for flavor)

Mix the dry ingredients thoroughly and add enough milk to make a stiff batter. Spoon the batter into the boiling broth until the entire top is covered in batter. Cover tightly. Reduce the heat and simmer for 10 minutes — do not lift the lid during this time. While dumplings can often be wet and waddy, these came out light and fluffy.

Chapter 2:
Soup

For a long time before our boat became a reality, we looked to it as a dream of the ideal. It would be our chance to live life well. Now, years later, we still feel that way. Whether aboard for a weekend or a three-month haul, we like to feel we are living the best way we possibly can.

That is why we make all our own soups.

Besides being delicious, our soups are nourishing and they make use of leftovers. Thus they help us nourish body and soul, and avoid waste, two goals which for some reason always become more prominent when we are living aboard. And that is probably why you can almost always find us aboard.

We're not the sort of people who potter about the galley trying to find things to do. If it took a lot of time or undue thought to make soup, you wouldn't catch us doing it, at least not on a regular basis. However, it is so easy that we make soup almost every day of the week, and we enjoy making it as much as eating it.

A friend rowed over for lunch one day, and after spooning down two bowls full of beef and mushroom soup I'd made out of the previous night's supper, said, "I really should learn how to make soup." Never having made it, she didn't know how simple it can be.

Soups have the same kind of mystique to a cook that women have to a man: both are viewed as basic, quite wonderful, and slightly elusive. The difference is that no one has ever come to understand everything about women, but one can come to understand all about soups.

Our recipe for making any kind of soup has two parts:
1. anything goes;
2. let your taster be your guide.

Basically, a soup is broth and seasoning. The broth can be meat, fish, fowl or vegetable. The seasonings can be anything from a diced onion to chili powder to vinegar, and can include any number of leftovers such as rice, beans, noodles, tomatoes, and so on. You never get tired of your own soups. They're always different depending on the ingredients and leftovers you have on hand.

Bean Soup

Nothing tops *Bean Soup* for lunch, in our book. We always make extra beans for supper so that there will be some left for a good soup the next day. Gary is the master at making it. He loves to see leftover beans, and rushes through supper so he can get his soup simmering.

To ½ or 1 cup of leftover beans add enough water to make 2 big bowls of soup if there are 2 people, 3 if there are 3 people, and so on. The beans can be lima, pinto, black, kidney or whatever. Add a finely diced onion and stalk of celery or carrot. Add several shakes of soy sauce. Season to taste with salt, pepper, garlic powder and paprika. At this point, if he thinks it needs it, Gary will add a beef or chicken buillon cube. Simmer that night for 10 minutes, and again in the morning for 10 minutes. At noon, heat and serve. Garnish with grated yellow cheese, or dried or fresh parsley.

Vegetable Soup

The vegetables that were crisp and appetizing when you left port a week ago may no longer be the sort of thing you'd want to serve fresh on the table, but they will make a nourishing soup. Chop up anything and everything. For soup for 5 people, place 3 cups of water in a saucepan and start adding: 4 tomatoes, 3 carrots, 2 stalks of celery, ½ a head of lettuce, a handful of spinach, 1 large onion, ½ a potato. Bring to a boil and simmer for 15 minutes before tasting. Then add whatever seasonings you think it needs. If there is a piece of toast left over from breakfast, you might crumble that up and add it. You may think the soup needs a meaty flavor, in which case you can add 1 or more beef bouillon cubes.

Chicken Soup

I was on board a friend's boat recently and watched her boil 4 chicken breasts for 10 minutes, then debone them for a supper casserole and pitch the bones in the garbage. We stared at the juicy, still meaty bones for a moment, then looked at each other and both shouted "Soup!" at the same moment. We retrieved the bones and made a pot of the best chicken soup yet.

To Make The Stock (or broth):

Place chicken bones in a pressure cooker and cover with 4 to 6 cups liquid. If the chicken was boiled, as ours was, use that liquid. And if you have any water saved from boiling vegetables, use that as well. For soup for 4 people, use the bones of 4 chicken breasts, or all the bones of a 3-pound chicken, or the necks and backs of 2 chickens. Pressure cook at 15 pounds pressure for 10 minutes. Cool. Skim off the fat. Strip all the meat from the bones with your fingers. Discard the bones. (If you don't have a pressure cooker, bring to a boil and simmer for about 1 hour, until the meat falls easily from the bones.) This liquid with the bits of meat is the stock.

Taste the stock. It should have a definite chicken flavor. If it is too weak you have two choices: either add a bouillon cube or two, or boil away some of the liquid thereby concentrating your stock and making less soup.

To Make The Soup:

To the stock add any seasonings that you think might improve the flavor. If you're not sure of any particular one, add just a bit of it, taste, add a bit more, and continue from there. One day I might add only salt and garlic. Another day, soy sauce, garlic and pepper. Or salt, garlic, paprika and a hint of curry.

Then add other things. I always add a finely-diced onion, and quite often a diced carrot for color and vitamin A. Try one or any combination of the following: celery, rice, beans, broccoli, spinach, tomato (not too much). I keep some mixed dried vegetables on board in case I don't have anything interesting or fresh from the store to add to my soups.

Simmer until all ingredients are soft.

Serve, not boiling hot, but at a temperature of about 170°F.

Egg Drop Soup, which always looks very fancy and tricky but which is easy and fast, is a variation of *Chicken Soup.* It is best to use stock that has very few other additions. If your soup turned out full of chunks of meat and vegetables, strain most of them out.

Beat 1 egg very well. Bring broth to a boil. Stirring broth rapidly with a fork, slowly pour egg in a fine stream over the fork. The egg cooks as soon as it drops into the soup, creating that speckled effect.

Serve with a few fresh peas or freshly chopped green onions as a garnish. This works very well in *Lipton's Chicken Noodle* dry soup mix. And in a pinch you can make your stock out of 3 bouillon cubes in 2 cups of boiling water.

Onion Soup

Onions are an ideal shipboard food because they keep so well, they are nutritious (high in potassium and magnesium, substantial amounts of vitamins A and C, some calcium and several trace minerals) and because they add fast and easy zest to many meals.

The first time I had homemade onion soup was on *Isla's* maiden voyage way back in 1974, somewhere in the Sargasso Sea on our way to Miami. Nancy Brock, one of the crew, explored the bilge on the first calm day we'd had since departing New York, and discovered that what had been cold storage in Lake Ontario had turned into a steamy hothouse. Garden produce was rotting. She pulled out the onions, peeled off the mushy outside layers and converted the still good parts into a huge cauldron of savory soup.

4   **medium onions (for soup for 4 people)**
3   **tablespoons butter (margarine or vegetable oil will do)**
4   **beef bouillon cubes (or pan drippings from a roast of beef)**
¼   **teaspoon pepper (freshly ground is superior)**
    Parmesan cheese

Slice onions thin and sauté until browned in the butter. Add 4 cups water, bouillon cubes and pepper. Bring to a boil and simmer for 5 minutes. Serve and sprinkle with Parmesan cheese. Each bowl can be topped with a rusk (see index) or croutons before sprinkling with the cheese. Make extra and store in a thermos for the night watch.

Lentil Soup for Two

Lentil soup is filling. The lentils have substantial quantities of carbohydrate and protein, are high in phosphorus and potassium and have sizable amounts of vitamin A and calcium. They are not widely used in North America for the simple reason that we did not grow up with them — they are not part of our culture. But they make a fast base for soups and main course dishes and keep forever on board ship in an airtight container. As a staple for long-distance sailors, they are worth investigating.

½   **cup dried lentils**
¼   **pound beef (ground or in chunks)**
1   **tablespoon tomato paste or 1 tomato, diced**
1   **onion, chopped**
1   **beef bouillon cube**
1   **teaspoon molasses (sugar will do)**
1   **teaspoon vinegar**
½   **teaspoon chili powder**

Soak the lentils all morning in 1¾ cups water. This increases their nutritional value, but does not substantially decrease the cooking time, so soaking is not essential. Fry the beef until well browned and add to the lentils, using some of the water to get all the browned, flavorful drippings in the frying pan. Add everything else. Bring to a boil and simmer for 15 minutes. Serve and garnish with paprika, parsley, or grated yellow cheese.

Split Pea Soup

Split peas also keep forever on board in an airtight container, and make a hearty, tasty soup for a cool day.

½   **cup split peas**
3   **cups water**
2   **tablespoons butter**
    salt

Soak peas overnight in the water. Boil for 45 minutes, or boil for 10 minutes and then pressure cook for another 10. (The boiling first gets rid of the froth that might clog the air vent in the lid of the pressure cooker.) Add butter and salt. Taste. You might like to add a beef or chicken bouillon cube. Garnish with bacon bits.

Beef Noodle Soup

I discovered recently that homemade noodles are easy to make, tasty, and are an alternative to bread and soda crackers.

1   cup flour (white or whole-wheat, or a combination)
3   eggs (or several egg yolks)
1   tablespoon milk or water

Mix ingredients together until the batter is smooth and pliable. Divide the dough into 2 balls and roll out on a floured board. Make it as thin as you possibly can. Cut into ribbons and drop into a pot of boiling beef broth. Or, if you have the space and the time, the rolled dough can be dried for several hours until dry but not stiff, at which point it can be rolled up and sliced — this makes the slicing less tedious and the noodles more even. Or you can pat the ball into a rectangle shape, about 8 x 4 inches, and about ¼-inch thick, and cut off big fat noodles. I have a friend who simply spoons little balls of the batter into her soup.

The thin noodles need only a few minutes to cook in the boiling soup. The fat noodles take 6 minutes, and the balls 10. To make the beef broth, add 3 beef bouillon cubes to 2 cups boiling water.

Pumpkin Soup

Vitamin A is essential for good health, and vital for a sailor's night vision. The body's supply can be quickly depleted, so we need some intake daily — this is sometimes difficult, especially on board ship. Pumpkin and squash are excellent for supplying the required vitamin A.

1   cup cooked pumpkin or squash
1½ cups water or milk
1   tablespoon butter
1   tablespoon brown sugar
¼   teaspoon salt

Push the pumpkin through a sieve if you have cooked it yourself. This isn't essential if you don't have a strainer on board, but it does make a more finely-textured soup. Add all the ingredients. If you can't decide whether you want a water or milk-based soup for your first try, make it with water, taste, then add 2 tablespoons milk powder to ½ cup and taste again.

Heat, but do not boil (to prevent milk from congealing, if you use milk base). Try a touch of allspice or nutmeg. If you prefer a thicker soup, you may want to use just 1 cup of water or milk.

Fish Or Seafood Chowders

Chowders are a meal in themselves and can be served as the main dish.

- 1 **pound (approx.) fish, conch, clams, etc. for 4 people**
- 1 **medium onion, finely diced**
- 1 **tablespoon butter or bacon grease**
- 1 **tablespoon flour**
- 1 **large potato, diced**
- 2 **cups milk**

Simmer fish in 1 cup water until flakey. (Conch must be beaten first until almost falling apart, then finely chopped.) Sauté onion in butter or bacon grease until brown. Sprinkle flour over onions and stir until blended, then add to fish, potato and milk. Heat, but do not boil, until potato is tender. Taste. You may want to add salt, another tablespoon of butter, or a touch of garlic powder. Garnish with parsley or paprika. Like all recipes, this one is flexible, and you may want to sauté a few chopped green peppers with the onions, or add a finely diced carrot or two along with the potato.

Dumpling Soups

Any kind of soup can become a dumpling soup. It's a great idea for a boat because it makes a fast, one-pot meal. Just drop spoonfuls of dumpling batter (see index) into a fast boiling soup, put the lid on, turn the heat down and simmer for 10 minutes. When I take the pot to the table and remove the lid, the skipper on our boat is always pleased and surprised and exclaims "Dumplings!" as if it were a special treat and I had gone to more trouble than usual. If the truth were known, I had gone to *less* trouble.

Exotic Tinned Soup

Tinned soups are fast, and most boaters stock a wide variety. With very little effort, they can be doctored to improve their flavor and appearance, increase their nutritive value, and astound one and all with your creativity. To plain old cream of tomato soup you can add a finely diced onion, a few shakes of soy sauce and a touch of garlic powder, and sprinkle Parmesan cheese on top. I always add a beef bouillon cube or two to pea soup. Add a small can of tinned chicken to chicken noodle soup, and garnish liberally with chopped green onions. Add croutons (see below) to beef broth and chopped chives to cheese soup. Add a finely chopped leftover pork chop to cream of mushroom soup. Add 2 teaspoons lemon juice, a touch of garlic powder and 1 tablespoon sherry to onion soup, and top with croutons. Chopped spinach, romaine or broccoli can be used as ingredients or garnishes. The options are endless.

Croutons

Slice bread into ¾-inch cubes. Sauté, turning frequently, in butter, margarine or bacon grease, until golden brown on all sides.

*   *   *

Chapter 3:
Salad

Salads, like soups, can be concocted from almost any combination of foods. There is no rule. A salad may be hot or cold, fresh or tinned, fruit or vegetable, carbohydrate or protein, jellied or tossed, bite-sized chunks or finely diced, sweet or sour, or any combination thereof.

Common ingredients for salads are: lettuce, romaine, onions, green onions, tomatoes, carrots, cabbage, green peppers, potatoes, noodles, beans, olives, walnuts, sunflower seeds, sprouts, ham, bacon, chicken, eggs, cheese, celery, apples, pickles, parsley, oranges, grapes, grapefruit. But you might also try: avocado, papaya, sesame seeds, almonds, coconut, broccoli, cauliflower, well-fried ground beef, beets, corn, pears, watercress.

We always have two dressings on our table, and they are always the same two. I prefer *oil and vinegar* on almost all salads, while Gary prefers *mayonnaise.*

Oil and Vinegar Dressing

¾   **cup oil**
¼   **cup vinegar**
¼   **teaspoon salt**
¼   **teaspoon garlic powder**

Mix and shake. I am usually in a hurry, which is why I use garlic powder, but 1 or 2 crushed cloves of garlic provide a superior flavor. Any vegetable oil will do. I find all olive oil too strong, but ¼ cup of olive oil and ½ cup corn oil is a good combination. Brown cider vinegar has a more mellow flavor than the white. Try substituting lemon juice for vinegar, or use ½ lemon juice, ½ vinegar. One beaten egg yolk added produces a more viscous texture and more mellow flavour — and greater nutritive valve.

Mayonnaise Dressing

This recipe was described in the section on how to live without refrigeration (see index). When we are on land, we do put it in the fridge, but that isn't necessary.

1　**can sweetened condensed milk**
½　**cup vinegar**
¼　**cup water**
1　**teaspoon salt**
1　**teaspoon mustard powder**

Dissolve the mustard in the vinegar. Put all ingredients into the jar in which you intend to keep the mayonnaise, and stir with a spoon until it thickens. To cut down further on the dishes, and the ship's water, measure vinegar and water in the tin that the milk was in. The measurements do not have to be exact.

Following are our favorite salads on board ship.

Alfalfa Sprout Salad

We have this two or three times a week, and all it consists of is a big bowl of alfalfa sprouts, and nothing else. We like both the short, new sprouts, and the older ones with the small green leaves. Gary eats them with no dressing at all, but I put on my usual sprinkling of *Oil and Vinegar*, and Parmesan cheese.

Mung Bean and Carrot Salad

Combine equal quantities of mung beans (we prefer the young ones) and grated carrot. It is good served with either dressing.

Brazilian Cabbage Salad

This is a variation on coleslaw. Chop or shred the cabbage. Add ½ as much Brazil nuts, finely chopped, as cabbage. The Mayonnaise Dressing is best with this salad.

Rice Salad (1)

This consists of equal quantities of cooked cold rice and diced greens — such as Chinese cabbage, broccoli or spinach — and a finely chopped onion. It is good with either oil and vinegar or mayonnaise dressing.

Rice Salad (2)

When you are short of fresh greens, use 1 small tin of corn and 1 tin of green beans, a few chopped olives and a finely chopped onion.

Avocado and Tomato Salad

Avocados are not a great ship board item because they go bad as soon as they are ripe. However, I buy them whenever I get the chance because they contain more vitamins and minerals than any other fruit, and because we both like them. When the avocado is ripe (very soft and starting to turn black), cut in half, peel off the skin and cut into wedges about ¼-inch thick. Cut tomatoes in wedges. Place avocado and tomato wedges alternately on a plate and sprinkle the juice of 1 lemon over the whole plate. Sprinkle very lightly with salt.

Guacamole

This is a Spanish word, pronounced "wakamolay", with the accent falling on the "mo." Avocado, the main ingredient, comes from the Aztec "ahuacatl" or testicle tree. The Aztecs considered it to be an aphrodisiac — however, I cannot confirm (or deny) this. Sometimes for lunch we will have this avocado salad with toast and nothing else. *Guacamole* also makes a good chip dip.

    1   **very ripe avocado, finely chopped**
    1   **small tomato, finely chopped**
    1   **small onion, finely chopped**

**1   tablespoon lime juice
salt and pepper to taste
a few shakes of Tabasco sauce, or cayenne pepper**

Mix thoroughly with a fork. Eat immediately: it turns brown if allowed to sit.

Gazpacho

Ordinarily the ingredients for this are made into a soup, but we prefer it as a salad. It is very refreshing. Chop equal quantities of tomato (not fully ripe), green pepper, onion and cucumber (optional). Oil and vinegar dressing goes best with this.

Waldorf Salad

Chop 1 cup of celery and 1 cup of apples, and add ½ cup of chopped walnuts. Serve with mayonnaise dressing. This is also good with dried apples in place of fresh.

Cucumber-Sour Cream Salad

I never get enough of this one. Slice a cucumber and purple onion. Stir 2 teaspooons lemon juice, 1 teaspoon sugar and ¼ teaspoon salt into 8 ounces sour cream. Gently mix all together.

Canned Tomato Salad

Mix together 1 can drained tomatoes cut in eighths, 2 coarsely chopped eggs, 2 teaspoons mayonnaise, and salt and pepper to taste.

Dill Pickle Salad

Mix all together with a few tablespoons mayonnaise: 3 dill pickles, chopped; 3 hard-boiled eggs, chopped; 3 or 4 pimentos, chopped; 1 small onion, sliced; and 2 tablespoons ketchup.

Potato Salad

Cook 4 extra potatoes at supper for potato salad for lunch the next day. Make the salad that night, as it is better if it marinates at least 8 hours. Dice the potatoes. Stir in ½ cup of mayonnaise and sit overnight. Just before lunch add a diced onion, a stalk of celery, chopped, and a few sliced radishes. Place in a serving bowl and garnish with slices of 2 or 3 hard-boiled eggs.

Tuna Salad

Mix together 1 tin of tuna, 1 chopped onion, and whatever else you have, like spinach or bean sprouts or green peppers. Add 2 teaspoons vinegar and 3 tablespoons mayonnaise.

Noodle Salad

Boil 8 ounces noodles for a salad for 4 people. Drain and cool. Add 1 chopped onion, a few chopped pimentos, ½ cup chopped almonds, and a small tin of corn. Squeeze the juice of 1 lemon into it. Add ½ cup of mayonnaise and mix gently. Garnish liberally with parsley.

The Everything Salad

Several boats were having a cookout on the beach, and it fell to the lady from the 22' sloop to bring the salad. She had no fresh produce on board, but nonetheless came up with a big bowl of crunchy salad we could all enjoy. She used approximately equal quantities of these canned foods: corn, green beans, garbanzo beans, and kidney beans. She threw in a small jar of pimentos, a larger one of mushrooms and a handful of sunflower seeds. She also added ½ pound crumbled bacon. Finally, she diced 4 slices of bread, fried them crispy brown, and stirred them in at the last minute. The dressing she brought was oil and vinegar.

Pineapple-Cabbage Salad

    2   cups cabbage, finely chopped
    1   cup marshmallows
    1   tin pineapple, cut into small chunks
    1   small tin water chestnuts, diced
    ¼   to ½ cup chopped walnuts
    ½   cup mayonnaise

Mix all ingredients and let sit for ½ hour before serving.

A Note on Growing Sprouts

Some boaters have trouble with sprouts, especially alfalfa, rotting before they have fully grown. All sprouts must be rinsed 3 or 4 times a day, and the water drained off. They grow best in a closed space from which moisture cannot readily escape. A 3-pound peanut butter jar with screening over the mouth for draining the sprouts is used successfully by some people. I use a bowl in a plastic bag and catch the seeds in a strainer when rinsing. There is always a small percentage of alfalfa sprouts that do not sprout, and these stay in the bottom of the bowl or jar and start to rot. I remove these the third day of sprouting by adding a cup or so of water to the sprouts, swirling — which allows the unsprouted seeds to float loose and settle — and then lifting the mass of sprouted seeds out. This reveals the unsprouted culprits lying on the bottom, and they are then easily removed.

Chapter 4:
Main Course

The One-Pot Meal

Whether a weekend boater or live-aboard, you often need a fast meal that can be eaten from a bowl or a mug in the cockpit, and which requires a minimum of cleanup. The one-pot, stove-top meal fits the bill. It is ideal if you're out in any kind of weather, if you'd rather spend time with dinner guests, or if you want to finish scrubbing the growth off the boat's bottom. The one-pot meal becomes a specialty for many boaters because it so well fits almost any occasion.

The pressure cooker is the perfect pot for these fast meals because the thick bottom prevents burning and keeps the contents hot for an hour or so — which means that people can eat in shifts, or that supper will still be hot if a sail change is needed just as everyone sits down at the table.

The one-pot meal is more easily consumed if it is fairly thick in consistency. A too-thin one-pot meal can be quickly thickened by adding to the pot and stirring in a slice or two of bread, fresh or stale, crumbled. This may sound somewhat crude to you, but it is a time-honored, seaman-like practice dating back centuries. Broken bits of ship's biscuits were added to soups and meat dishes to thicken them, provide carbohydrates and make use of any otherwise unusable food.

Described below are twenty-one one-pot meals. They are examples only — ingredients can be switched around or substituted to make other dishes.

Tuna-Noodle Casserole for Two

8   ounces elbow noodles (about 2 cups)
3   cups water
1   tablespoon vegetable oil or bacon grease
6½ ounces tuna
1   tablespoon dried onion chips, or 1 fresh onion, diced
1   teaspoon vinegar or lemon juice
½   teaspoon salt
1   tin green peas, or 1 cup chopped broccoli, or anything green
    pepper and garlic powder to taste

Boil noodles in water and oil, covered, until soft. Blanching is not necessary. Drain off excess water, if any. (So as not to waste the water supply, I try to calculate the exact amount of water needed. Sometimes I have to add a bit more to the pot before the noodles are done.) Add all the other ingredients. Mix gently. Heat over low heat for 5 minutes. If you like a creamy texture, add ½ cup milk powder. To save fuel and further time at the stove, turn the burner off when you add the ingredients, and just let sit for 5 minutes. All ingredients will be hot but at a more edible temperature.

Beef-Noodle Casserole for Two

½   pound ground beef
8   ounces noodles, shell or elbow
3   cups water, part of which is liquid drained from the tomatoes
1   tablespoon oil or margarine
2   beef bouillon cubes
1   tablespoon dried onion chips, or fresh onion, diced
12 ounces tinned tomatoes, drained
1   teaspoon chili powder
½   teaspoon salt
1   tablespoon dried green peppers, or 1 fresh green pepper, diced, or anything green
    pepper and garlic powder to taste

Fry beef until well browned. Boil noodles in water, tomato juice and oil until soft, by which time they should have absorbed all the liquid in the pot. Crumble bouillon cubes and dissolve in 1 tablespoon boiling water. Add bouillon and all the other ingredients to noodles. Mix gently. Let sit for 5 minutes.

Cottage Cheese Casserole for Three

This is the same as *Beef-Noodle Casserole*, except you add 8 ounces of cottage cheese to the noodles along with everything else. This makes a stickier dish, as the cheese melts a little and becomes cohesive. You can make it without the tomatoes too.

Macaroni and Cheese for Four

1	pound elbow noodles
6	cups water
2	tablespoons butter, vegetable oil or margarine
1	pound sharp yellow cheese, grated or finely chopped
2	tablespoons dried onion chips, or 2 onions, diced
1	cup milk powder
	parsley
	salt, pepper and garlic powder to taste

Boil noodles in water and butter, covered, until soft and until they have absorbed all or almost all water in the pot. Add all other ingredients and let sit for 5 minutes. Garnish liberally with parsley, fresh or dried.

Mulligan for Two

I was brought up on this as a child, as was my mother, whose father used to make it for his three little girls after his wife died. He, too, was a sailor, hailing from the Isle of Man. Perhaps this recipe came from his shipboard days. Mother says that there is probably another name for this dish, "but that's what Daddy called it."

4	medium potatoes, scrubbed, not peeled
2	cups liquid, water plus potato water
½	pound ground beef, well browned, drained of grease

1   beef bouillon cube
1   onion, diced and sautéed
1   stalk celery, or any other vegetable
    salt and pepper to taste

Slice potatoes ¼-inch thin or thinner, and boil until tender but not mushy. Add 2 cups water (using the potato water for part of this) to the browned beef, salt, pepper, onion and bouillon cube. Mix. Thicken by dissolving 2 tablespoons flour in ½ cup water and stirring into the boiling meat mixture. Simmer and stir until thick. Add potato slices and vegetable. Remove from burner and allow to sit for a few minutes so that the vegetable will heat through.

Beef Stew for Four

1   pound beef, cut into bite-sized chunks (if cheap cut, tenderize first with tenderizer, or pressure cook at 15 pounds pressure for 15 minutes)
4   medium potatoes, cut into chunks
4   carrots, thick slices
8   small onions, whole
2   stalks celery, in bite-sized chunks
3   tablespoons tomato paste
3   cloves garlic, crushed
1   teaspoon chili powder
2   beef bouillon cubes
2   tablespoons flour
    dash of vinegar and soy sauce
    salt and pepper to taste

Brown beef in frying pan with a bit of oil. Place all ingredients except flour in pot, cover with water and bring to a boil. Simmer until vegetables are tender, about 15 minutes or place in pressure cooker and steam at 15 pounds pressure for 4 minutes. Dissolve flour in ½ cup water and stir into liquid in pot. Adjust flavor. You may want to add more bouillon cubes.

Chicken Stew for Six

Half the quantities for *beef stew*, leave out the chili powder, tomato paste and vinegar, and substitute 1 pound chicken for the beef, and chicken bouillon for the beef bouillon. Fry the chicken in a frying pan and then debone. Or pressure cook at 15 pounds pressure for 15 minutes and debone. Cut into chunks. The juice in the bottom of the pressure cooker is then used for part of the liquid to cover the vegetables.

Chicken Fricassee for Four

5   pound chicken, cut into pieces
1½ cups water
2   carrots, sliced
1   onion, sliced
4   potatoes, diced
2   tablespoons flour
    salt, pepper and garlic powder to taste

Pressure cook chicken at 15 pounds pressure for 15 minutes in 1½ cups water. Take down from pressure and add carrots, onion and potatoes. Bring up to pressure again for 7 minutes. Bring down from pressure and thicken gravy with 2 tablespoons flour dissolved in ½ cup water. Adjust flavor. This looks quite gala if sprinkled with tinned mushrooms and parsley just before serving.

Chicken Pot Pie

This is *chicken stew* with a biscuit crust. To make the crust you will need:

1   cup flour
1½ teaspoons baking powder
¼   teaspoon salt
1½ tablespoons shortening
¼   cup milk

Mix all together and roll out on a floured board to fit the size of your pot. Bring stew to a boil, place crust on top and turn down to a low heat. Keep covered for the 15 minutes cooking time.
This can be *beef pot pie* if you use beef stew for the base.

Ham and Egg Noodles for Four

1   pound egg noodles
6   cups water
1   tablespoon vegetable oil
1   pound tinned ham, cut into bite-sized chunks
16 ounces of corn

¾   **cup water**
1   **tablespoon soy sauce**
1   **tablespoon brown sugar**
½   **teaspoon vinegar**
1   **tablespoon butter**
1   **teaspoon cornstarch (or 2 of flour)**

Boil the egg noodles in the water and oil until soft, by which time most of the water will be absorbed. Drain off excess water. Remove from heat and add the ham and corn. Make a sauce with the ¾ cup water, soy sauce, brown sugar, vinegar and butter. Dissolve 1 teaspoon cornstarch or flour in the mixture and then bring slowly to a boil, stirring constantly, until thick. Pour sauce over noodles and ham. Mix gently.

Chili for Two

½   **pound ground beef, well browned**
16 **ounces kidney beans**
1   **large onion, diced and sautéed, or 1 heaping tablespoon onion chips**
1   **green pepper, diced and sautéed, or 1 tablespoon dried green peppers**
1   **small tin tomato paste**
16 **ounces tinned tomatoes**
2   **cloves garlic, crushed**
1   **tablespoon or more chili powder**
1   **tin mushrooms, optional**
1   **tablespoon sugar, optional**
1   **teaspoon vinegar**
    salt and pepper to taste

Combine all ingredients. Simmer 10 minutes to allow flavors to meld. Garnish with fresh chopped green onions and/or Parmesan cheese. You can use ½ pound fresh mushrooms instead of the tinned, in which case, cut them in half and add to all the other ingredients for the 10 minutes simmering time.

Congri for Four

This Cuban dish is a complete meal without meat, even though many people from northern climates feel they're not well-fed unless they have eaten flesh of some sort. A pound of well-browned beef can be added to the *Congri* recipe and perhaps a beef bouillon cube or two. Or you might add a tin of chopped ham. Or even three or four leftover wieners chopped up or sliced. Often a thick slab of cheese on top is the answer — it is delicious as it melts down into the beans and rice below.

½ **cup black beans**
½ **cup rice**
1 **tablespoon bacon grease**
1 **teaspoon cumin**
1/8 **teaspoon cayenne pepper**

Soak black beans at least 4 hours, preferably overnight (to reduce the cooking time). Pressure cook at 15 pounds pressure in water to cover for 12 to 15 minutes. Or boil for about 1 hour until tender. Add the rice, 1½ cups water, bacon grease and seasonings. Bring up to pressure again for 5 minutes for white rice, 8 minutes for brown. Or boil about ½ hour until rice is soft. Serve as is, or add any meat. Garnish with grated yellow cheese.

Spanish Rice for Four

¼ **to ½ pound bacon, cut into bits**
½ **cup rice**
½ **cup onions, thinly sliced**
20 **ounces tinned tomatoes**
½ **teaspoon salt**
1 **teaspoon paprika**
1 **green pepper, finely diced**

Sauté the bacon until brown. Fry the rice in bacon drippings until brown. Add the onions and fry until brown. Add all other ingredients and steam in the double boiler for about 1 hour, stirring frequently. Or pressure cook rice at 15 pounds pressure for 5 minutes in 1 cup water to which you have added 1 tablespoon bacon grease, then bring down from pressure and add all other ingredients. Let sit in hot pot for ½ hour, or until the green peppers have cooked and the flavors have melded. You may need to add a few minutes of heat before serving. A towel wrapped around the pot will keep contents at a high temperature longer.

Wieners and Beans for Three

20 **ounces tinned pork and beans**
6 **wieners, tinned or fresh**

1   onion, finely diced
1   stalk celery, finely diced, or any green tinned
    vegetable
    soy sauce
    salt, pepper, garlic powder to taste

Boil wieners 3 minutes and discard water. Add all other ingredients and mix. Simmer for 5 minutes. Adjust flavor.

Ham and Beans for Four

1   stalk celery, diced
20   ounces tinned pork and beans
1   pound tinned ham, chopped into bite-sized chunks
12   ounces tinned tomatoes, drained
1   large onion, diced
½   teaspoon dry mustard
     soy sauce
     salt, pepper, garlic powder

For a quick dish, place all ingredients in pot and simmer for 5 minutes. For a little different flavor and for people who prefer the sautéed effect of onion and celery, sauté the onion and celery first in the frying pan in a little butter or vegetable oil, then place all ingredients in pot and simmer for 5 minutes. Serve with Parmesan cheese or ketchup.

Frijoles Refritos for Two

This is a common dish in Mexico, and there are many different ways to prepare it. Frijoles is the Spanish word for beans, and is pronounced "freeholays." Refritos means refried.

20   ounces tinned kidney beans
¼   to ½ pound mild, white, brick cheese, depending on
     how much cheese you like
1   onion, finely diced
½   teaspoon chili powder
     salt, pepper, garlic powder

Heat kidney beans, either whole or mashed, in a frying pan with the onion and seasonings. Lay slices of cheese over beans and put the lid on for a few minutes or until the cheese begins to melt. Serve with Tabasco sauce. Tortillas are the traditional accompaniment.

Lima Beans and Cheese

This is a variation on *Frijoles Refritos*, but not as quick because you must prepare the beans yourself. We find lima beans very tasty and satisfying, and have them about once a week when we're aboard.

2 **cups cooked lima beans (see index)**
1 **onion, diced**
¼ **to ½ pound yellow cheese**
6 **strips bacon, cut into 1-inch strips and fried until crisp**

Add onion to hot limas. Spread over beans and close lid for a few minutes, or until cheese starts to melt. Serve and garnish with bacon bits. If the lima beans are juicy, sometimes I add ½ cup milk powder to 2 tablespoons of the juice, then stir this milky mixture into the beans for a creamier texture.

Salmon Loaf for Two

½ **cup milk**
2 **slices bread, fresh or stale, crumbled**
2 **eggs, beaten**
7 **ounces tinned salmon (about 1 cup)**
1 **small tin corn (about 6 ounces)**
1 **tablespoon lemon juice**
salt and pepper to taste
Grated rind of 1 lemon (optional, but it is a very savory addition)

Heat but do not boil the milk, and add the crumbled bread. Mix well. Add the eggs while still warm, and stir well. Add all other ingredients and mix. Pack into a greased, 20-ounce tin and cover with aluminum foil or small lid and pressure cook at 15 pounds pressure for 20 minutes. Or pack into 2 greased 14-ounce tins and pressure cook for 15 minutes. Bring pressure down. Open bottom of tin with a can opener. Slide a knife around the eggs and push loaf out. For a very casual meal, or on a rough night, eat straight from the tin.

Dumplings

As described in the section on breads (see index), these make a hearty one-pot meal and can be used over any kind of a stew base. Therefore you can make beef, chicken, chicken liver, lamb, or even chowder dumplings. And the dumplings themselves can be varied by adding such things as grated cheese, parsley, sesame seeds, allspice, or by using different combinations of flour.

Dumplings are often used to stretch a meal. Half a pound of beef chopped into small bits will make an adequate meal for four if served as dumplings. You may feel that the protein content is not adequate, so use some soy flour in the dumpling batter, but not more than 25 percent. Or you can stir several tablespoons of soy flour into the gravy. Soy flour has no gluten and will not thicken the gravy — you must use white or whole-wheat for that.

Beef Stroganoff for Four

1	to 1½ pounds fillet, or thin steak, pounded with a mallet until even thinner, then cut into 3-inch long strips about 1-inch wide
4	tablespoons butter
1	small onion, very finely diced
1	pound sliced mushrooms, or 8 ounces tinned, drained
¼	cup white wine
1	cup sour cream (or 1 cup double-strength powdered milk with 1 tablespoon vinegar added)
1	pound egg noodles
6	cups water

Boil the egg noodles until tender in water to which has been added about 1 tablespoon of the butter (or vegetable oil) to keep the noodles from sticking. Meanwhile, in a frying pan sauté the beef and onion in 1 tablespoon of the butter for about 5 minutes, turning the beef to brown both sides. Remove from pan and melt remaining 2 tablespoons of butter in the pan, then sauté the mushrooms until slightly browned. Add all ingredients to the hot noodles and mix gently. In place of the white wine, you can use ¼ cup of the liquid from the drained tinned mushrooms.

Beef and Lentils for Two

¾	cup lentils
2	cups water
½	pound ground beef, well browned
½	tin tomato paste

12   **ounces tinned tomatoes, drained**
1   **onion, diced, or 1 tablespoon dried onion chips**
1   **green pepper, diced, or 1 tablespoon dried green
pepper**

Simmer lentils in water for about 20 minutes or until soft. Drain off excess liquid. Add all the other ingredients and let sit for 5 minutes. Serve with Parmesan cheese or Tabasco sauce.

* * *

More Elaborate Meals

Tuna or Salmon Patties for Two

6½   **ounces tinned tuna or salmon, or ½ pound fresh
tuna or salmon, cooked**
1   **medium onion, finely diced**
1   **egg, beaten**
1   **teaspoon lemon juice or vinegar
salt, pepper, garlic to taste
enough flour to make the mixture sticky, about 2
tablespoons or bread crumbs**

Mix all ingredients thoroughly. Shape into about 6 balls, press flat, and fry in a medium hot pan in bacon grease or vegetable oil until crispy brown. Serve with lemon wedges, and perhaps mashed potatoes and pickled beets.

Dried Fish Patties

Every now and then you hook a fish that is big enough to fill the cockpit. This elicits great shouts of glee and triumph, until some unkind soul asks, "But what do we do with it all?" It can be a problem, especially on boats that have no refrigeration. Even on boats that do, fresh fish is best when it is only hours old, and yesterday's catch may be discarded in favor of a more recent one.

Try to dry the fish in the rigging where it is exposed to the wind and sun, by scoring it deeply every inch or so and sprinkling it lightly with salt. The salt draws the juice from inner areas to the surface where it evaporates. Native peoples around the world do this. It takes only a few days and once dried, will keep for ever.

This dried fish flesh makes delicious fish cakes. Simply reconstitute the fish in a bit of water by letting it soak for an hour or two. Break it up with a fork and add the same ingredients as you would for *tuna patties*. This can be done whether the fish has been drying for three days, or three months.

Deep-fried Fish for Four

When we are in the Bahamas, where Gary goes spear-fishing almost every day, one of our favorite suppers is grouper fingers with beans and rice. The fingers batter (or the deep-fried batter) performs a minor miracle in that it allows you to feed a multitude of people with a small catch.

Gary's mother gave me this batter recipe, and she got it from Lillian — but for the life of her she can't remember who Lillian is. The name stuck — however, and the recipe is known as *Lillian's Fish Batter*. You wonder how such a simple batter can taste so good, but it does. Many people ask me for the recipe, and are always surprised to find that there's no secret ingredient. The only secret may be that the batter doesn't mask the mild flavor of the fish.

1   **cup water**
1   **cup flour**
2   **teaspoons baking powder**

Mix flour and baking powder thoroughly. Add water and stir lightly. Cut 1 to 2 pounds fish into "fingers" about 1 x 3 inches. Pat them dry if they are wet and slippery, so that the batter will stick. Dip each finger into the batter. Drop fingers into hot but not smoking oil and fry until crispy golden brown. If you don't like to use that much oil, put 2 to 3 tablespoons oil in a hot frying pan, place batter-coated fingers in pan and brown first one side, then the other. However, the fish will not remain as moist if fried this way.

Smelt

"The smelt are running!" is an exultant cry that is as much a symbol of promise as the rainbow. Smelt is surely one of the most joyful delicacies of spring on the Great Lakes and an unmistakable sign that Nature's bounteous wealth has returned full cycle once again.

Early in May, watchful townsfolk head down to the lakes

and creeks that feed them to look for the return of the smelt. If they see a few, they come back the next day with a net and pail and sit on the pier to wait with other watchers. Then one day, there are millions of smelt, and you can get all you want in minutes.

One year, operating on a hot tip, four of us took a large smelt net and drove to a creek near Port Hope, Ontario. In less than an hour, we caught — to our amazement — hundreds upon hundreds of fish as they swarmed upstream from Lake Ontario. The large garbage can we'd brought was soon full, and the two men could barely lift it into the truck.

Cleaning the smelt took the four of us two hours, but we dined all the while on freshly fried ones as they sizzled, pan after pan, on the stove right beside us. They were tender, moist, sweet, and had that incredibly light and clean flavor that only very fresh fish can have.

Fresh smelt are left to air dry 5 minutes each side, or are patted dry with a paper towel. This drying helps the batter to stick. Each fish, held by the tail, is then dipped into the following batter:

1   **egg, well beaten**
½   **teaspoon soy sauce**
½   **teaspoon garlic powder**

The smelt are then rolled in flour. Whole-wheat is very good (a little crunchier than white and more nutritious, of course), but white is fine. If you have a lot of smelt to do, put 1 cup of flour in a paper bag, toss in the smelt and shake. Then place the smelt in a very hot but not smoking skillet into which 3 to 4 tablespoons of oil have been poured. They are delicious without lemon or vinegar, but the acidity is nice for variety. When eating smelt, some of our friends leave the tail like the core of an apple. However, the tail is our favorite bit — always a very crisp and tasty morsel, something like a gala potato chip.

What did we do with the hundreds of smelt that we couldn't stuff into our bulging bellies that night? We froze some — just plopped them into plastic bags in one-meal portions, and crammed them into the small freezer. They kept very well for several months (until they were gone) and were much better tasting than the frozen ones you can sometimes buy in the supermarket. Why this is so, I don't know — unless it was their super freshness at the time of freezing.

We smoked the rest of the smelt in a canvas teepee six feet high, using elm and scrap lumber left over from some building projects. We stored them on a long string over the dining area where they got drier and drier, fishier and saltier, and chewier — quite like the dried cod that is served in restaurants in Nova Scotia. We enjoyed them with beer.

Lobster

The secret, if any, to good lobster is the butter-garlic sauce. And the secret to butter-garlic sauce is two-fold. First, don't burn the butter, melt it over low heat. Second, it needs lemon juice.

Butter-Garlic Sauce

¼	**pound butter**
4	**cloves garlic, crushed**
	Juice of 3 lemons
	Dash of salt

Melt the butter. Add the garlic and sauté lightly for 1 or 2 minutes. Add the lemon juice and salt. Serve in the same pot in which it was heated, to keep it hot longer. Reheat as it cools. Dip chunks of lobsters into the sauce before eating.

For the lobster itself, it's hard to go wrong. Clean the intestinal tract by inserting an antennae into the anus and twisting. When the antennae is pulled out, the entire intestine should come with it. Place tail, claws, antennae bases and, if the lobster is a large one, the antennae and legs, in a pressure cooker and bring up to 15 pounds pressure for 4 minutes. Or put into a pot, cover with boiling water and boil for 15 minutes. Split tails with a chopping knife. We use pliers for the legs and antennae, but I'd understand if you'd rather use nut crackers, or even the specially adapted lobster crackers. Serve hot, with rice and salad.

Lobster-Grapefruit Salad

Sometimes when you're cruising down south and eating a lot of lobster, you wish there were some new way to eat the stuff. Well, there is! We discovered this quite by accident one day when Gary speared a particularly big lobster. We ate all we could that night, and there was still half left for morning. As we had several grapefruit on board, it was clear that breakfast should be an experiment. The lobster and grapefruit just turned out to be a heavenly combination.

1 **pound cooked lobster, cut into bite-sized pieces**
1 **cup grapefruit sections, cut in half**
6 **to 8 maraschino cherries, cut into quarters (these are not essential but they do add color)**
½ **cup mayonnaise**
½ **cup sour cream or yogurt**

Gently stir all together. Serve cool rather than ice cold to better appreciate the subtle flavors. We use our own mayonnaise (see index), but you can use Miracle Whip. The sour cream/yogurt can be replaced with another ½ cup of mayonnaise, or with sour cream substitute (double-strength powdered milk with 1 tablespoon lemon juice or vinegar).

After discovering this salad, we came across a similar one in a 1930's Florida cookbook, but it called for 1 cup of halved green grapes instead of grapefruit. This, too, is refreshing.

Conch

Tough is the first word that comes to mind when many people think of conch. Yes, it is, if you don't beat it. No matter how you prepare conch, beat it first. Then it can be as tender as scallops. Even when you intend to grind the conch for fritters, it needs to be beaten first to relax the muscle - otherwise you might as well advertise them as leather fritters. Use a mallet, or a piece of wood. About three minutes per conch does the trick.

Conch Fritters for Four

1 **large conch, or two small ones (beaten!)**
1 **onion, finely diced**
1 **tablespoon green pepper, finely diced**
1 **tablespoon lime or lemon juice**
salt, pepper, garlic powder to taste
a few shakes Tabasco sauce, or tiny bit of cayenne pepper
fish batter or dumpling batter, using 1 cup flour for 4 people

Mix together all ingredients, and drop spoonfuls of the batter into hot grease. Let cook until golden brown. Serve hot with beans and rice.

Ceviche

Ceviche (pronounced seveechee) with the accent on the "vee", is raw fish marinated in acidic liquids. The flesh turns white and flakey so that it looks and tastes cooked. It is delicious and refreshing. You can use conch, or any kind of fish. It can be served as an hors d'oeuvre or salad if there is only a little, or as a main dish if there is more. Gary has become the ceviche master on our boat, and won't let me touch it.

> 1   **pound fish or conch (beaten!), cut into small, bite-sized pieces**
> 1   **cup acidic liquids - a good combination is ½ cup lemon juice or vinegar and smaller amounts of tomato and orange juice**
> 1   **onion, sliced**
> 1   **green pepper, diced**

Combine all ingredients and let marinate 1 to 2 hours. Adjust the flavor. If too acid, you may want to add 1 tablespoon sugar and 1 tablespoon water. Garnish with a diced tomato. Serve with beans and rice if it is a main dish, or with macaroni and cheese if it is a salad or hors d'oeuvre. It is good as a mid-afternoon snack, too.

Sweet and Sour Chicken for Two

This was the first meal I ever made for Gary. Now I make it whenever I want to serve something special.

> 1   **small chicken, cut into pieces**
> ½   **cup brown sugar**
> ¼   **cup vinegar**
> 8   **ounces tinned pineapple chunks, save juice**
> 8   **ounces tinned mushrooms, save liquid**
> 1   **tablespoon butter**
> 1   **medium onion, diced**
> 1   **green pepper, diced (or 1 tablespoon dried green peppers)**
> 1   **tablespoon soy sauce**
> 3   **cloves garlic**
> 1   **chicken bouillon cube**

Fry chicken until golden brown, but not necessarily until chicken is done. Remove temporarily from pan and add the juice from the pineapple chunks and mushrooms, the soy sauce, brown sugar, butter, vinegar and bouillon cube. Stir until sugar is dissolved. Sauté onion, green pepper and garlic, and add to sweet and sour sauce in frying pan. Put chicken pieces back into pan, turn heat to medium and simmer until chicken is done and sauce has thickened to a syrupy texture. Turn chicken several times to prevent sticking and to allow sweet and sour flavor to permeate the chicken. Add pineapple chunks and mushrooms at the last minute and let heat through. Serve in a casserole dish and garnish with something green — I like chopped green onions if I have them, but I have also used dried parsley, chives, chopped broccoli or spinach.

Quick Fried Chicken for Ten

Use three 4-pound chickens cut into pieces, not counting the necks and backs — save them for soup.

Pressure cook the chicken in two loads in a pressure cooker at 15 pounds pressure for 5 minutes. This does not completely cook the chicken, but it greatly reduces the cooking time in the frying pan. This step can even be done the day before, or any time during the day before supper. Then at supper time, it is a simple matter to merely brown the chicken — it saves you having to slave over the stove while company is there.

Put 3 to 4 tablespoons oil in a hot frying pan (use two pans if you can borrow one for the night) and fry until golden, about 5 minutes each side. Serve with potato salad prepared in advance.

Corn Beef Fritters

These were described in the section on time-saving tips (see page 70).

Pizza

This was described in the section on stove-top cooking (see page 56).

Fondue for Four

The only time I have ever been served cheese fondue was in Montreal during an exchange weekend with the University of

Montreal known as "Le Weekend Carabin." That year, 1964, the staff member accompanying the French-Canadian students was Pierre Trudeau, who was then teaching law. After numerous cultural and political discussions, we were served this fondue by Michel Gouault, an intense, red-headed historian, who spent all afternoon preparing it for the sixty of us. It was such a superb finale to a fascinating day that I grilled Michel on its preparation. I have never forgotten it and have served it occasionally on the boat as a special meal for charterers on their last night on board.

1   **pound Gruyère cheese, grated**
3   **cups dry white wine**
3   **tablespoons Kirsch (cognac will do)**
1   **tablespoon cornstarch**
1   **loaf Italian or French crusty bread, cut into 1-inch**
     cubes
1   **teaspoon paprika**

In a thick-bottomed saucepan, heat the wine over medium heat, uncovered. In a small container, dissolve the cornstarch in the kirsch. When the wine is simmering but not boiling, slowly add the shredded cheese, stirring constantly. Continue stirring until the mixture starts to thicken. Then, stirring more quickly, add the Kirsch and cornstarch mixture. Cook and stir for another few minutes until the mixture has thickened. Add the paprika. Transfer the pot to the table, and place over an alcohol lamp if you have one. If not, reheat if it cools before it has been eaten. Issue forks. Serve with bread cubes and a plate of fresh fruit that can be eaten with fingers or forks.

Beef Heart

Sometimes I serve beef heart sheerly for the pleasure it gives me when, at some point during the meal, I ask people if they know what they're eating and they look up, curious that I should be asking. Someone says tentatively, "Well, it's roast beef, isn't it?" "Nope," I say triumphantly, "It's beef heart." They are always amazed.

Beef heart is one of the best buys there is. There is practically no fat through or around it. The average 2-pound heart has less than an ounce of wastage. It has greater quantities of the B vitamins than does steak, three times as much iron as liver and much more magnesium, phosphorus and potassium than liver. It slices easily, keeps well, cans well, and makes a very tasty gravy.

Preparation is easy. Place whole heart in pressure cooker with about 1 cup water at 15 pounds pressure for 20 minutes. then slice very thin and serve as you would beef — with gravy and mashed potatoes, or on bread (as a hot heart sandwich). Or it can be sliced thin and then into strips for beef stroganoff.

To make the *Hot Heart Sandwich*, lay several slices of thinly sliced heart on bread and smother with gravy. Garnish with parsley. Serve with potatoes and vegetable.

Roast of Beef

First sear roast on all sides in a frying pan with a bit of oil to seal in juices and flavor, and then prepare as above for *Beef Heart*. Or, slice to about 3 inches thick and "roast" in frying pan with the lid on, about 20 minutes each side. Potatoes cut in half, and carrots cut in chunks, can be done at the same time for the whole 40 minutes in the frying pan, or in the pressure cooker by adding them to the pot for the last 5 minutes cooking time. Make gravy from the juice in the bottom of the pressure cooker as for heart gravy, or from the drippings in the bottom of the frying pan by adding 1 cup water to the pan (with roast and vegetables removed) and using a wooden spoon to dissolve the drippings in the water. Thicken with flour as for *Beef Heart Gravy*. Adjust flavor if necessary with salt, garlic powder or a bouillon cube.

Wieners with Cheese

Allowing about 3 wieners per person, tinned or fresh, slice wieners in half lengthwise, leaving enough uncut casing on bottom to hold halves together. Place them cut side up in the frying pan and lay strips of yellow cheese on both halves of each wiener. Fry over a medium high heat, covered, for 2 or 3 minutes, or until cheese starts to melt and wieners are browned on the bottom. Serve with French fries and a vegetable, perhaps beet pickles.

Spaghetti and Meat Sauce for Four

This is an old standby and fast to make if you've got a jar of canned hamburger in the bilge. If not, and there's no corner store behind the next wave, make it without meat and serve a little extra cheese.

1   jar (about ¾ pound) canned hamburger
2   cloves garlic, crushed and minced
20   ounces tinned tomatoes
1   tin tomato paste
2   beef bouillon cubes
1   teaspoon salt
¼   teaspoon pepper
1   bay leaf
1   teaspoon vinegar
1   tin mushrooms
1   tablespoon chili powder
1   tablespoon sugar or molasses

Place all ingredients except mushrooms in a thick-bottomed pot, bring to a boil and simmer for 15 minutes, or bring up to 15 pounds pressure for a few minutes. If you are starting with raw hamburger, brown it first, drain off the grease and then proceed. Add mushrooms just before serving. Serve over spaghetti noodles (¼ pound per person), with a salad and grated cheese, either Parmesan or sharp Cheddar.

Simple Spaghetti

Lew McGregor assured us that Italian friends of his often served this on board as an authentic Italian dish. All you do is prepare the spaghetti, and serve it with *butter-garlic sauce*, prepared as for lobster (see index). Serve with salad and cheese.

Meat Loaf

This always seems quite gala to us, like a roast turkey does on shore.

1   pound ground beef (or ¾ pound canned hamburger)
2   eggs
2   tablespoons dried parsley
½   stalk celery, diced
1   medium onion, diced
½   cup bread or cracker crumbs
2   tablespoons ketchup or tomato paste
       a few shakes soy sauce
1   tablespoon bouillon cube dissolved in 1 tablespoon hot water

½ teaspoon sage
¼ pound ground cooked liver (beef or pork) is a savoury addition if you have it, but by no means essential
salt, pepper, garlic powder to taste

Mix everything thoroughly. If too juicy to form a cohesive loaf, add as many tablespoons of flour as necessary. Melt 3 to 4 tablespoons bacon grease or lard in a frying pan over medium-low heat. Shape meat mixture into loaf and place in frying pan, covered, for about 20 minutes each side. Serve with a seasoned tomato paste spread on top. Good with fried potatoes and tinned tomatoes.

Hamburger Sauce for Two

½ pound ground beef, fresh or canned
¾ cup water
1 beef bouillon cube
1 medium onion, diced
1 tablespoon flour
salt, pepper, garlic powder to taste

Brown the beef and drain off the grease. Add all other ingredients except the flour, sautéing the onions first if you prefer (Gary does, I don't). Bring to a boil. Dissolve the flour in ¼ cup water and add slowly while stirring. Cook until thickened. Serve over bread rusks or mashed potatoes, with a vegetable.

Chapter 5:
Vegetables

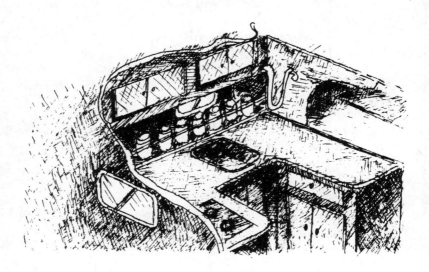

There is no substitute for fresh vegetables, either in flavor or nutritive value. On a boat they are at a premium because of lack of storage space for fresh produce, and because you are sometimes not within rowing or walking distance of markets. Therefore, boaters hate to discard any part of them and often eat and relish parts that are usually considered inedible. This includes radish leaves, cabbage hearts, cauliflower leaves, beet tops, beet stems, celery leaves, green pepper centers and seeds, cucumber skins, squash skins, potato skins, watermelon ring (like zucchini), apple cores and peach pits.

These usually-discarded items are highly nutritional, which is why boaters, anxious to have as complete a diet as possible, will eat them. Much of the nutrition in a cucumber and a potato, for example, is just under the skin — the part that is ordinarily thrown out. All seeds contain many vitamins and enzymes, which are the requisite for starting new life. And vegetable leaves contain, among other things, valuable amounts of vitamin A, important for night vision and healthy skin.

Most boaters look twice at anything vegetable before they demote it to the rank of refuse. If it looks at all edible, they will experiment with it. Et voilà — sautéed corn silk, and corn cobs flambé! Hm-m, I wonder...

Most vegetables are delicious and more nutritious when served raw — either in chunks as finger foods (with or without a dip) or as a salad. Fresh sweet corn is a superb addition to almost any salad. *Guacamole* (see index) is a good vegetable dip, as are any of the regular chip dips.

To cook vegetables, it is usually just a matter of heating until they are tender, and serving with butter. Pressure cooking, steaming or sautéing is the best way to retain nutrients and flavor; it is preferable to boiling in water to cover. Here are a few tips for specific vegetables.

Spinach, Beet Tops, or Other Greens

For about 10 ounces of greens, bring 3 tablespoons of water to boiling in a frying pan. Add washed greens and spread out more or less evenly. Put lid on and boil for 3 minutes. The greens cook perfectly like this and use a minimum of water. Serve with butter, salt and vinegar.

Squash

Cut into halves or quarters and place in a pressure cooker with about 1 cup of water. Bring to 15 pounds pressure for 5 minutes. Bring down from pressure, scoop onto plates and top with butter.

Creamy Mashed Potatoes

Cut 4 cleaned, unpeeled potatoes into quarters and pressure cook at 15 pounds pressure for 5 minutes in about ¾ cup water. Bring down from pressure and mash potatoes until smooth with the remaining water — a wooden spoon will do if you didn't stock a potato masher. Mix 1 tablespoon flour with ½ cup milk powder and stir into the steaming potatoes — it will thicken in less than a minute. Stir in 1 or 2 tablespoons of butter.

This method of preparing mashed potatoes means no water wastage, no vitamins poured down the sink, no garbage, and all that time saved by not peeling. Some people say that for company they like to serve the whitest potatoes possible, so they peel them for guests. But I say that for company I like to serve the best nutrition possible, so I leave the skins on. Neither Gary nor I has peeled a potato in over ten years.

Potato Patties

Make extra mashed potatoes so that you'll have some left over to make patties the next day. To a cup or so of mashed potatoes add a beaten egg and a small onion, finely diced. Shape into patties with your hands and place in a medium hot pan with some oil or bacon grease until crispy brown. The egg is optional, but adds protein if you need it for that meal.

Potato Rolls

This recipe also uses up leftover mashed potatoes. Mix together a cup of mashed potatoes, ½ cup flour, 1 egg, and 1 teaspoon baking powder. Shape into balls and "bake" in a frying pan over medium heat, in melted butter or bacon grease, using 1 flame tamer. Flip to brown the other side.

Carrots

Sprinkle 1 or 2 tablespoons of sherry or lemon juice over hot carrots, then butter before serving.

Creamed Corn from Dried Corn

Last winter, Gary's mother mailed us, along with other goodies in her Christmas care package, some corn that she had dried. I had previously tried some dried corn from a natural foods store and thought it was dreadful stuff, so it was not with great anticipation that I set some of Iola's to soak — in spite of how she had raved about it being such a treat when she was a child. Creamed dried corn continues to be prepared and relished by people of Pennsylvania-Dutch extraction, of whom Gary's mother is one.

This corn of Iola's, true to her word, turned out to be delicious, sweet and tender. It offers a tasty alternative to tinned corn on the boat.

Plunge young corn cobs into boiling water for 3 minutes, then quickly into cold. When cool, cut kernels off the cobs, and spread on cookie sheets which have been covered with brown paper. Place cookie sheets in the oven at the lowest possible heat. Dry until they are shrivelled and they rattle when moved. The drying can be started in the oven and finished under a hot sun for a day or two, or it can be done completely outdoors as long as there is a full day of sun to get it started. Iola remembers the kernels being stored in paper bags when she was a child, but I keep mine in a plastic bag where they store well for the month or so it takes to use them up.

To prepare corn for eating, soak for a few hours, then boil for a few minutes. To cream, remove some of the liquid and dissolve 1 teaspoon of cornstarch (for 2 people) in the liquid. Return it to the pot, stirring until thickened. Add some milk powder and a lump of butter. Stir and serve. Or add liquid milk to drained, cooked corn, and thicken.

Lima Beans

    1   **cup dried baby lima beans**
    2   **cups water**
    1   **tablespoon butter or margarine**

Soak limas 4 hours or more in the 2 cups of water. Pressure cook at 15 pounds pressure for 8 minutes, or boil until tender, about 1 hour. Bring down from pressure, add butter and stir. For variety, add a small tin of mushrooms. Garnish with parsley, or grated yellow cheese.

*   *   *

Tricks for sprucing up Tinned Vegetables

Tinned Spinach

"Yuk!" I thought one day when a friend served us a heap of very dead tinned spinach. But I was surprised at the good flavor when such spinach is served with butter and vinegar. I still enjoy it that way, but like it even more as spinach soup. Add 1 tin of water to the tin of spinach in a pot. Add 2 beef bouillon cubes, ½ teaspoon salt, 1 teaspoon butter and 2 teaspoons of vinegar. Heat and serve. Garnish with Parmesan cheese.

Tinned Tomatoes

Add a small onion, minced, ½ teaspoon lemon juice, a shake of allspice, and salt and pepper. Serve hot or cold.

Tinned Green Beans

Heat and top with bacon bits or grated yellow cheese.

Tinned Carrots

These, more than any other tinned vegetable or fruit, go bad, sometimes after a few months. Be sure to check the tin before opening, and discard it if puffy. Glaze the carrots to enhance the flavor. Discard the water from a 12-ounce tin of carrots and add to a hot frying pan 2 teaspoons butter and 2 tablespoons brown sugar. Stir in carrots until they are coated, and heat until the liquid becomes syrupy and all the carrots are glazed.

Pickled Beets

Pour off half the liquid from a tin of beets and replace it with vinegar. Add 1 tablespoon brown sugar and a dash of salt. Mix and let marinate for at least ½ hour.

Creamed Vegetables

Any vegetable can be glorified with a cream (or white) sauce. Besides adding variety, and in my case bringing a smile to the skipper's face, using a sauce is a way of stretching a dish if you're short.

- **2 tablespoons butter**
- **2 tablespoons flour**
- **1 cup milk (fresh or from powder)**
- **¼ teaspoon paprika (not essential, but we like it)**
  salt and pepper to taste

Melt the butter. Add flour and stir until smooth. Slowly add the milk, stirring constantly, and cook until thick. Add seasonings.

Cheese Sauce

Cheese is a delicious addition to many a vegetable dish, and is particularly suitable if your meal is lacking other protein. Just add 1/3 cup grated sharp cheese to the hot creamed sauce (above), and stir until melted.

Instant Creamed Vegetables

Some people call this cheating, but I prefer to call it cutting corners. Simply pour 1 can of undiluted cream of mushroom soup over steaming hot vegetables. If the vegetables are not extremely hot, heat the soup first. Intensify the flavor of the soup (or sauce) by adding a dash of soy sauce, parsley or Parmesan cheese.

Chapter 6:
Desserts

Tinned Peaches

There are all manners of tinned fruits that deserve a spot in the
bilge, but one that holds a special spot in many a sailor's heart
is peaches — tinned or canned. They have a peculiar ability to
soothe a queasy stomach. During rough weather once, on a
New York to Miami passage, four of us could not eat for two
days — and not eating doesn't make you feel any better. The
weather abated somewhat, but food would still not stay down.
Suddenly I remembered the peaches that Gary's mother had
canned. I crawled to the galley bilge and dug out a quart. They
were glorious — sweet and cool — and the four of us rejoiced
that they were staying down. Somehow, they were exactly
what our stomachs craved. I dug out another quart, and we
demolished it as well.

Clare Francis, in her book *Come Hell or High Water*,
reports that during her single-handed trans-Atlantic crossing,
tinned peaches were for her, too, an antidote for an unsettled
stomach. Whether it's the high vitamin A content or the
potassium or what, I don't know and don't really care.
Peaches work, and that's all that counts.

We never eat them any other way — just straight from the
quart jar, completely unadulterated. They are best in a thin

rather than a heavy syrup. Gary's mom uses half sugar, half honey, and I'm sure her canned peaches can't be topped. (See index for canning instructions.)

Pineapple Upside-Down Cake

1½   cups sugar
½   cup butter (margarine or shortening will do)
2   eggs, beaten
1   teaspoon vanilla
2¼   cups flour (half oat flour is good)
½   teaspoon salt
2   teaspoons baking powder
1   cup milk (made from powder)

Topping:

1/3 cup butter or margarine
¾   cup brown sugar
     pineapple slices or chunks

Cream sugar and butter or shortening. Add eggs and vanilla, and beat until fluffy. Mix flour, salt and baking powder thoroughly. Add flour mixture alternately with milk to the sugar mixture, beating well after each addition. That is the cake.

For the topping, melt the 1/3 cup butter in a frying pan, sprinkle the brown sugar evenly over the butter and arrange drained fruit over the bottom of the pan, in the sugar-butter mixture. You can also add some sliced almonds. Pour cake batter over the fruit. "Bake", covered, over medium low heat with a flame tamer for 20 to 30 minutes. Or, if you have an oven, bake at 350°F for 45 minutes. It is done when a knife inserted in the center comes out dry. While still hot, turn upside-down on a plate. You may have to arrange the fruit a little, or cut pieces out of the cake from the frying pan and turn them upside-down as they are served onto individual plates. Good with cream, or double-strength powdered milk.

Dried Apple Upside-Down Cake

Same as above recipe for pineapple, but use 2 cups dried apples reconstituted for about 1 hour in a cup or so of water or fruit juice. Again, the flame tamer is essential to prevent burning.

Rice Pudding the Easy Way

If you are ever marooned on a desert island, be sure to take ashore with you lots of rice and several tins of sweetened condensed milk. During the twelve days on the island after the shipwreck, the six of us had this rice pudding many times for dessert, and it was always a treat.

2   to 3 cups leftover rice (we used brown)
½   cup raisins
2/3 tin sweetened, condensed milk

Add the raisins and condensed milk to the still warm rice and let marinate from 4 to 12 hours. Serve with cream, which can be made from the remainder of the sweetened condensed milk diluted with an equal amount of water.

Pie Crust for One 9-inch Pie

1   cup flour
½   teaspoon salt
1/6 cup shortening
2½ teaspoons cold water

Mix thoroughly flour and salt. Cut in shortening with knife, fork, or pastry blender until mixture is crumbly. Add water and mix. Roll dough into a ball that is easily manipulated. Roll out on floured board using a bottle if you haven't stocked a rolling pin. Fold crust in half to transport it safely to the pie plate. Unfold, and pinch dough around the edge of the plate. For a pie that calls for a *baked pie crust*, prick the bottom several times with a fork to prevent bubbles, and bake on a raised rack in the pressure cooker-canner (without the ring, and not under pressure) for ½ hour, or in the oven at 350°F for 40 minutes.

Key Lime Pie

(see index)

Pumpkin Pie

Unlike most other pies, *Pumpkin Pie* can be considered part of the main course because it is full of nutrients. Pumpkin and squash are high in vitamin A and potassium, the milk is high in calcium, phosphorus and protein, and the eggs are high in iron, vitamin E and protein.

Pumpkin pie is really squash pie — while pumpkin can be used, squash makes the more flavorful pie.

The last time we had *pumpkin pie*, Gary made it by adding his own smashing touch: rum flavoring. Talk about heaven! The rum is a natural, as it blends smoothly with the cream and spices. Our lunch that day was pumpkin pie, lots of it, and nothing else.

2	**cups squash, boiled and pushed through a strainer (or 1 tin pumpkin pie filling)**
1½	**tablespoons flour**
1-2	**cups milk (or evaporated milk)**
1	**cup brown sugar, well packed**
1/3	**cup rum**
2	**eggs, slightly beaten**
1	**teaspoon salt**
1½	**teaspoons cinnamon**
1½	**teaspoons allspice**
½	**teaspoon cloves**
	up to 1 tablespoon molasses, if you prefer your pie dark brown
	nutmeg grated from a fresh seed

Mix all ingredients except nutmeg thoroughly and pour into unbaked pie shell. Sprinkle with nutmeg. Bake at 350°F for 40 minutes, or until a knife inserted comes out clean. Or, place pie on raised rack in pressure cooker-canner and bake over medium heat for ½ hour. Or, spread pie dough into thick-bottomed small frying pan and "bake" over low heat, with 1 flame tamer, for ½ hour.

Bananas

When you stock up for your one or two-week vacation on the boat this year, you may include a big hand of firm, yellow bananas. What a perfect boat food. Handy for snacks or breakfast fruit, needs no washing, nutritious, and a good source of vitamin A, potassium and magnesium, the banana has more vitamin B1, B2, B6, folic acid and niacin than a raw egg yolk — always listed as a particularly good source of the B vitamins. There are small amounts of sodium, phosphorus, calcium, iron, copper, selenium and zinc. It is higher in trace minerals than most other fruits. And because it has some vitamin C, the banana will help keep scurvy at bay.

The one drawback to this meritous monkey food is that all the bananas ripen at the same time. No sooner have they changed from green than, presto, they're black. They are not rotten or inedible at this point, but they do look unsavory, and many people don't care for that overly sweet flavor that a fully ripe banana has. However, it is at this stage that they are ideal for four delicious desserts: fritters, bread, pudding, and flambé.

Banana Fritters

(see index)

Banana Bread

(see index)

Banana Pudding

(no cooking)

Mash 2 very ripe bananas with a fork until smooth. Add the yolks of 2 eggs and mix. Beat the egg whites until stiff, adding 1 teaspoon of sugar when they are half whipped. Fold in whites. Top with grated coconut. Serve with cream if you like. Eat immediately — the egg whites lose their froth after a while.

Banana Flambé

The pièce de résistance is always *banana flambé*. It sounds exotic, looks exotic, but there is nothing tricky about it. It once saved the day for us when we had eight charter guests couped up inside the main salon while it blew and howled the very devil of a gale outside. I started the flambé right after lunch and it sparked great interest. Everyone dove into it chortling and jostling each other for more. (I do suspect that my success had something to do with the bottle of rum I had to open for the recipe — it somehow never got put away.)

2   **ripe bananas, cut in half lengthwise**
¼   **cup lime juice (lemon will do)**
½   **cup brown sugar**
¼   **cup butter**
¼   **cup rum**

Melt the butter in a frying pan. Add sugar and lime juice and mix. Place bananas in pan. Simmer for 5 minutes or so, or until the liquid has become a syrup. Turn the bananas carefully once or twice so that they brown on both sides. Bananas should be covered with a thick sauce when done. Remove from stove and take to table. Pour rum over bananas and light with a match. It will burn gently with a blue flame for a minute or two. Vanilla ice cream is a good accompaniment.

There are two desserts which will help use up bananas before they are ripe. One is sliced bananas served with brown sugar and cream, the other is bananas and oranges chopped and mixed with brown sugar, using equal quantities for the two fruits. An old English shanty celebrates this latter dish, appropriately called "Bananas and Oranges."

Dried Apple Fritters

Reconstitute dried apple slices, about 10 per person, in a bit of water, for 15 to 30 minutes. You can put them in a bowl and turn every minute or so, so that each slice is regularly exposed to more water. Or lay them out on a flat plate and sprinkle water over them. Drain off excess water and use it for the liquid in the fritter batter (see index).

Doughnuts

1	egg
½	cup sugar
½	cup milk
2	tablespoons melted shortening
2	cups flour
2	teaspoons baking powder
¼	teaspoon salt
¼	teaspoon allspice
1	teaspoon grated lemon or orange rind

Beat the egg and slowly add the sugar, beating constantly. Stir in the milk and melted shortening. Mix thoroughly the flour, baking powder, salt, allspice, and grated rind, and add this flour mixture to the wet ingredients, mixing briefly. Drop tablespoons of the batter into hot grease and deep fry until golden. Let cool for a few minutes, then drop into a paper bag that has ½ cup icing sugar and shake. (The icing sugar is optional.)

Prickly Pear Upside-Down Cake

When you go ashore for a day's exploring in warmer parts of the world, you sometimes come across a huge patch of the thorny prickly pear cactus, with its deep purple fruits, about 1½ x 2 inches, perched helter skelter on the branches. These fruits make excellent eating either fresh, in jams, or in this cake that I made once for a cookout on the beach on Stocking Island in the Bahamas, which was attended by twenty-some-odd boaters (some odder than others).

Dessert is often a neglected part of the sailor's menu — he or she is too busy beachcombing, hullscraping or swapping sea lies to find the time. Anyway, everyone knows it's not good for you. But at the famous Stocking Island cookout, I cut this prickly pear dessert into about twenty-five pieces and had a good laugh as the diet-conscious boaters loaded up their plates with the dessert, sometimes two pieces, *before* they reached for the rice and driftwood-grilled fish.

Pick the prickly pears with heavy gloves — it is best to wear something impermeable, like rubber. Rub off the fine hairs — they are torture on the tongue. Peel about 20 for this dessert. Add about 1½ cups of water and boil for a few minutes. Push through a strainer or collander to remove the seeds. Add 2 tablespoons butter, let melt, and stir in. Pour into a greased frying pan. Pour the cake batter (same as for *pineapple upside-down cake)* over juice. "Bake" over medium low heat, covered, using 1 flame tamer, for about 20 minutes.

Cookies

Almost any bar-type cookie or squares that are ordinarily baked in a pan can be done in the frying pan on top of the stove. Here are two of our favorites.

Brownies

½	**cup butter or margarine (vegetable oil in a pinch)**
1	**cup brown sugar**
1	**egg**
½	**cup cocoa**
½	**cup flour (whole-wheat is excellent)**
	dash of salt
¼	**teaspoon baking powder**
½	**to 1 cup chopped almonds or walnuts**
1	**teaspoon vanilla**

Cream the butter and sugar. Add the egg and mix well. Combine the cocoa, flour, salt and baking powder and add to the first mixture, mixing well. Add vanilla and nuts. Spread into a greased medium-sized, thick-bottomed frying pan and "bake" over medium low heat with 1 flame tamer for 15 minutes.

Shortbread

The recipe comes from my mother who always baked dozens and dozens of these for us every fall when we headed south on *Isla*. Many cool evenings at the helm were accompanied by a coffee and two or three (we doled them out to make them last) of these melt-in-your-mouth, wonderful cookies.

½	cup butter
3	rounded tablespoons sugar
¼	teaspoon salt
1	cup flour (whole-wheat, white or half and half)
1	teaspoon cold water
½	teaspoon vanilla
½	cup chopped pecans

Cream the butter well. Add sugar, a tablespoon at a time, and cream again. Add salt and mix in. Add flour and mix thoroughly. Add water and vanilla and mix thoroughly. Add nuts. This is where Mom and I part company. She shapes hers into little loaves, 1 x 2 inches, puts them on a cookie sheet and bakes them in the oven for 20 minutes at 350°F. I press mine into a frying pan, score into wedges to facilitate turning, and "bake" over medium low heat, uncovered, with 1 flame tamer, for 8 minutes each side, or until just slightly golden.

Date-Nut Loaf with Sauce

1	tin date-nut loaf
1	cup brown sugar
2	cups boiling water
2	tablespoons butter
1½	tablespoons cornstarch
1	teaspoon vanilla
½	teaspoon allspice
½	cup candied fruit

Melt the butter and add the cornstarch, stirring until smooth. Add the sugar and continue to stir over heat until the mixture turns a darker brown — about 5 minutes. Slowly add the water and cook 1 or 2 minutes until the mixture becomes thick. Stir in the vanilla, allspice and fruit. Remove the date-nut loaf from its tin and steam 5 minutes or so until hot. Slice into 6 servings and pour the hot sugar sauce over the individual portions. For real decadence, top with whipping cream.

Fudge

1	cup milk
2	cups sugar (we use 1 cup brown, 1 cup white)
1/8	teaspoon salt
2	ounces grated chocolate
3	tablespoons butter or margarine
1	tablespoon vanilla
½	to 1 cup chopped walnuts or almonds

Bring to a boil in a heavy pot (the pressure cooker is good) the milk, sugar, salt and chocolate, stirring constantly to dissolve sugar. Reduce heat and continue boiling, cooking to the soft ball stage (when ½ teaspoon or so of the fudge will form a cohesive ball when dropped into a glass of cold water for a few minutes). Add the butter and vanilla. Beat vigorously until the fudge loses its sheen. From here on in you have to move fast, or it will set up in the pot. In less than 30 seconds you must add the nuts, stir them in and pour the fudge into a waiting, greased pan. Cut while warm. Eat any time. Don't kill each other fighting over the pot.

Super Strawberries

We each have a special food that we dream about during a long passage, and then as soon as the anchor bites rush ashore to satisfy the craving. For some it is ice cream, for others, Coke. For me it is strawberries. I like them every conceivable way, (and even some inconceivable ways) but particularly smothered with calories.

1	quart strawberries
½	cup white sugar or mild honey
1	cup sour cream or whipped cream

Stem berries and cut into halves or quarters. Add sugar or honey and let sit for ½ hour, stirring occasionally. This brings out the flavor and makes a syrup. Add cream and mix gently.

Wait until the rest of the crew has gone ashore and serve. Mm-m.

Ron and Rhubarb Crisp

Boat building is almost as much a part of sailing as the sailing itself. This is partly because maintenance often requires rebuilding, and partly because without the builder, there couldn't be sailors. There *are* sailors, of course, who build their own boats, and for them the building and sailing are even more intricately intermingled.

We do not make *Rhubarb Crisp* on board because it really needs an oven. But it was a frequent dessert every spring while we were living at the barn and building *Isla*, — nearby grew an indestructable patch of rhubarb. I am including this recipe here because I associate it with boat building, and perhaps some of you will still be building; and also, because it was a favorite of Ron McGuire's. He was a man who loved the sea — especially the pretty blue of the Gulf Stream. One day in an effort to describe it to those of us who had never seen it, he said it was the prettiest, *prettiest* blue we would ever see. His eyes misted over, and we believed.

I never saw a man as crazy for *rhubarb crisp* as Ron. Every day that last spring he would say, in his beguiling way, "Hey, how about another rhubarb crisp tonight — you pick the rhubarb, I'll get the ice cream ...?" It was the "last" spring because we launched *Isla* that fall after six years of building, during which time Ron was almost always there. It was also Ron's last spring. He was lost at sea the following winter.

Ron was a life-sized version of a leprechaun. He was, in fact, Irish, with a mop of dusty-red hair and crinkles at the corner of his eyes that bespoke his constant good humor. To Ron, the world was made of good guys and bad guys, and even the bad guys deserved a laugh. He was a veteran seat-of-the-pants sailor, and made several epic off-shore passages, single-handedly, between Canada and the Bahamas. Just before he appeared to help us with *Isla* that last summer, he sailed his 50' catamaran alone from Miami to Weymouth, Nova Scotia, sailing up St. Mary's Bay after sundown. He ran the boat high ashore in what he hoped was the back yard of friends, stepped onto dry land and walked up to the back door proffering a can of peas, the only bit of food he had left. The friends hadn't seen him in years, didn't know he was coming, but made him more than welcome. Ron was welcome just about everywhere.

Shortly before his last trip, Ron's longtime girlfriend was killed in a diving accident in Lake Superior. Not much later, he lost his beautiful boat in a court quarrel. Nonetheless, it was Ron, who never lost the ability to see the humor in things, who kept me laughing that last hard spring and summer.

We rarely have *rhubarb crisp* any more, and I wish Ron were still around to pester me into making it.

3   to 4 cups pink rhubarb, cut into chunks
½   cup brown sugar
1   tablespoon flour

Topping:

½   cup flour
½   cup rolled oats
½   cup brown sugar
½   cup butter or margarine
1   teaspoon cinnamon
½   teaspoon allspice

Mix rhubarb, sugar and flour together and place in a buttered casserole or pan. Press down as much as possible. Mix flour, oats, spices and sugar for topping and cut in butter with a fork or pastry blender. Cover rhubarb with this crumble mixture. Bake in moderate oven until tender, about ½ hour.

Chapter 7:
Breakfast

Listed here are numerous suggestions for the morning meal. It's easy to get into a rut — not that there's anything wrong with a good, comfortable rut. But sometimes just seeing someone else's ideas can start you thinking about interesting variations on your own morning theme. I know, I know, there are people who don't like to think in the morning. The habit of groping about for familiar things in familiar places is a perfectly legitimate way to start the day, and anyone who prefers such a course should perhaps skip this chapter.

Certainly all these breakfast options were not available to our sea-going ancestors. They seemed to get by just fine on oatmeal porridge, which they called "burgoo," morning after morning. However, very few of these iron men with their stomachs of steel are still with us and it could very well be that this unvarying diet was the death of them. You will find recipes listed in this chapter for all the suggestions marked with an asterisk. (*)

French toast
Welsh cakes*
porridge — five varieties
doughnuts (see index)
fresh fruit and a roll

dried fruit, stewed, and bread
Johnny cake (see index)
pancakes
apple pancakes
elderberry pancakes*
rusks with peanut butter and apple sauce (see index for rusks)
bacon and tomato sandwich
fried egg sandwich
toasted Western
toasted egg salad sandwiches
fish patties
fritters* (apple, banana, etc.)
egg nog*
scrambled eggs
"Campbelled" eggs*
scrambled eggs with croutons*
quiche*
egg foo yong*
grilled cheese*
dried cereals, especially *All-Bran*
potato cakes*

* recipes following

Egg Nog

Beat 1 egg with a fork, whisk or egg beater until light. Strain. Add 1 or 2 teaspoons sugar or honey, a dash of salt, 6 ounces of milk and mix thoroughly. Sprinkle with allspice, cinnamon or nutmeg.

Banana Fritters

These are perfect for a slow morning when you feel like sitting around a bit. We recently had friends visit and the day they arrived there was a pile of bananas turning brown in the galley. Don and Sue got up early the next morning and started concocting a fritter batter, and by the time Gary and I stumbled out, there was a big plate of fritters already on the table. M-mm-m-m. We sat around and chatted and munched. Next morning it was my turn. And the third morning it was their turn again — there were still two tired old bananas left. By this time we had perfected the recipe, and these were the best yet.

1   **cup flour (½ oat, ½ wheat)**
1   **teaspoon baking powder**
3   **tablespoons sugar (brown)**
½   **teaspoon salt**
1   **egg, well beaten**
1   **cup milk (from powdered)**

Add sugar and salt to the egg mix. Add baking powder to flour and mix. Add flour mixture alternately with milk to the egg mixture. It should make a thick sticky batter that hesitates before running off a spoon. (You may need to add a touch more flour.) Cut bananas into ¾ inch chunks and dip in batter. Deep fry until golden. Let cool slightly, then drop into a paper bag that has ½ cup icing sugar and toss once or twice. Remove and serve. If you have insufficient oil for deep frying, the fritters are almost as good when done in a frying pan with just 2 or 3 tablespoons of oil, turning to brown the other side. They don't look quite as pretty, but then "pretty" isn't everything.

Elderberry Pancakes

Elderberry pancakes are without a doubt one of the most delicious and friendly ways to greet a new day. It has become a ritual with me to pick elderberries in mid-September and then to sun-dry them for use in winter when we are often sailing in the Bahamas. All summer I wait, watching the berries on the trees in the countryside turn from green to red to the rich purple-black that indicates the fruit is ready for harvesting. The birds, cleverly, also have been waiting and watching and will efficiently strip a tree overnight, so I never wait until the next day once I've seen the ripe berries. I pick as many as I can, which usually amounts to an 11-quart basket or two. Out of some I make a jam. But most I strip from the stems and spread on cookie sheets. I put them out in the sun for 5 to 6 days until the berries are hard and dry, tilting the trays to face the southerly set of the sun in September, and bringing them in at night to avoid the dew. Then I can hardly wait to make the first batch of pancakes.

> **1/3 cup dried elderberries soaked in 1 cup water for about 1 hour before breakfast. (If you haven't dried any of your own, you can get them at a health food store, but picking your own is half the pleasure of these pancakes.)**

2   cups flour (I use 1¼ cups white flour and ¾ cup soy flour to give extra protein)
1½ teaspoons baking soda
½   teaspoon salt
1   tablespoon sugar
1   egg, well beaten (the pancakes are fine without the egg, but it makes them a little firmer)
2   cups buttermilk or sour milk (I rarely have fresh milk on the boat, so I add ¼ cup of vinegar to 1¾ cups milk made from milk powder. You can use sweet milk in a pinch, substituting 3 teaspoons baking powder for the soda, but the acid improves the flavor.)
1½ tablespoons melted shortening or oil
1   tablespoon additional shortening

Mix together the dry ingredients. Strain the berries and stir them into the dry ingredients. Save the juice and use it for part of the water for making the milk. Add the beaten egg to the buttermilk, then add the melted shortening. Put a fat teaspoon of shortening into a hot frying pan. When it is melted and covers the entire bottom of the pan, spoon the batter into the pan. You may need to gently spread the batter out to the desired size if it is too thick to run out on its own. Fry over a medium heat until the top is done (dry), then flip and brown the other side. Serve with butter and honey, or maple syrup.

These pancakes are more filling than pancakes usually are, perhaps because of the soy flour. This recipe is ample for 4 to 5 people.

Scrambled Eggs

These are best done over a medium high heat, in butter, turning and mixing frequently. They should not be allowed to dry out as they are both easier to manage and have more flavor if still a little glossy. Pick up the flavor with a little salt, pepper and garlic powder. A teaspoon or more of Parmesan cheese adds a nice touch. Use about 1½ eggs per person. If making eggs for 4 and you have only 4 or 5 eggs, stretch them by adding 2 or 3 ounces of milk.

Scrambled Eggs and Croutons

Allowing about ¾ of a slice of bread per person, cut slices into ¾-inch cubes. Brown the cubes in a frying pan with a little butter or margarine, turning frequently to brown all sides. Remove from pan, keeping warm if possible. Scramble the eggs, and add the croutons when the eggs are not quite done, so that some of the egg batter will adhere to the croutons. Don't add them too soon, or the crisp croutons will become soggy.

"Campbelled" Eggs

So-called because of the use of a tin of Campbell's soup, this recipe idea also owes its name to the Campbells, the people who first served these to us. For *Campbelled eggs* for 4, add ½ tin of cream of chicken or cream of mushroom soup to 4 eggs and mix. Proceed as for scrambled eggs.

Egg Foo Yong

Our version is very simple, although I'm sure the official recipe is much more complicated. Sauté mung bean sprouts, about ½ cup per person, in butter over high heat for a few minutes. Add 4 beaten eggs and a few shakes of soy sauce and proceed as for scrambled eggs. Serve with soy sauce and fresh fruit, perhaps quartered apples.

Quiche for Four or Six

1	unbaked pie crust (see index)
½	to 1 cup shredded cheese
6	eggs
6	slices bacon
½	teaspoon pepper
1	tablespoon kirsch or cognac (not essential)
1	cup evaporated milk
	dash of nutmeg

Line a frying pan (or a pie plate if you have an oven) with the pie crust. Sprinkle cheese on bottom. Fry the bacon until it is not quite crisp, cut into 1 inch pieces and distribute them over the cheese. Beat the eggs and add the milk, Kirsch and seasonings and beat again. If you are short of eggs, use 4 eggs and 1½ cups milk. Pour milk and eggs over cheese and bacon. "Bake" over medium low heat using one flame tamer for about 20 minutes or until a knife inserted comes out dry.

Potato Pancakes (or Potato Latkes)

2   medium potatoes
1   egg
2   tablespoons flour
1   teaspoon salt
¼   cup milk
3   tablespoons lard

Grate raw potatoes on the coarse side of a grater so that you have long shreds. Quickly, before the potatoes turn black, add the egg, flour, salt and milk and mix. Drop spoonfuls of the batter onto a hot frying pan in which the lard has been melted. Use about 2 tablespoons of batter per pancake and spread it out until flat and fairly thin. Brown both sides. Potato pancakes are best when eaten immediately. Serve with sour cream, maple syrup or applesauce.

All-Bran

Constipation is not an uncommon problem among sailors. Chichester drank salt water daily as a preventative; other people exercise regularly. Some carry All-Bran, repackaged into plastic bags. This bran cereal is unquestionably both a preventative and a cure — as a preventative, ¼ cup per day; as a cure, a cup every hour until ... Delicious with cream and brown sugar.

Welsh Cakes

These biscuit-texture flat cakes are still served for breakfast in Wales. They are particularly well-adapted to the frying pan, and indeed the Welsh recipe calls for one.

3   cups flour (any combination, perhaps 1½ cups white, 1 whole-wheat, and ½ soy)
4   teaspoons baking powder
2   tablespoons brown sugar
½   teaspoon salt
1   cup shortening
¾   cup currants
1   beaten egg with enough milk to make ½ cup

Mix together the flour, baking powder, sugar and salt. Cut the shortening into this mixture using a pastry blender or fork. Add currants. Add egg and milk and mix. Form the dough into 2 balls, and knead each one 10 to 15 seconds, or until the lumps blend into one cohesive mass. Roll out each ball to ¼-inch thickness and to a slightly smaller diameter than your frying pan. Cut into quarters or eighths to facilitate turning. Lay the pie-shaped wedges into a lightly oiled frying pan, cover, and cook over medium heat using 1 or 2 flame tamers. Fry each side 6 to 7 minutes.

Instead of cutting into wedges, the dough can be cut into round cakes with a cookie cutter (or jar lid), but I've found that you must then do 2 batches for every dough ball, as they do not all fit into the pan.

Chapter 8:
Flotsam and Jetsam

Equipment:

1 teaspoon	5 ml (millilitres)
1 tablespoon (3 teaspoons)	15 ml
1/4 cup (4 tablespoons)	60 ml
1/3 cup (5-1/3 tablespoons)	79 ml
1/2 cup (8 tablespoons)	118 ml
1 cup (16 tablespoons)	237 ml
1 fluid ounce (2 tablespoons)	30 ml
8 fluid ounces (1 cup)	237 ml
16 fluid ounces (1 pint)	437 ml
32 fluid ounces (1 quart)	946 ml

Dry Measure:

0.035 ounces	1.0 g (gram)
1 ounce	28.35 g
1 pound	453.59 g or 0.45 kg (kilograms)
2.21 pounds	1 kg

How to Convert to Metric:

	When You Know:	You Can Find:	If You Multiply:
Mass:	ounces	grams	28.0
	pounds	kilograms	0.45

Liquid

Volume:	ounces	millilitres	30.0
	pints	litres	0.47
	quarts	litres	0.95
	gallons	litres	3.8
Temperature:	degrees F	degrees C	5/9 after subtracting 32

Sample Temperature Conversions:

Degrees Fahrenheit:	Degrees Celsius:
225	107
250	121
275	135
300	149
350	177
400	204
450	232
500	260

White Flour

White flour was an American invention designed expressly for the caravans of covered wagons heading west. Until a method was devised to remove the germ from the main part of the kernel, thousands of people arrived on the other side of the continent with their flour supply long since turned rancid. White flour filled a need, and was applauded. Unfortunately, the discarded germ, the part which sprouts when the seed is planted, contained most of the nutrition. It is especially rich in the B vitamins, vitamin E, protein, unsaturated fat, minerals, and iron and carbohydrates. The endosperm, the part we eat in the white flour, consists mostly of carbohydrates in the form of starch, small amounts of incomplete protein and mere traces of minerals and vitamins.

Whole-wheat goes rancid after a month or two because of the oils in the germ. For short term sailing, storing it is no problem. For long trips, white flour will keep practically forever in an airtight container. But a good diet is important, and at least some whole-wheat should be included regularly for more complete nutrition. Small amounts that will not go bad before they are used up can be replenished from time to time. For boaters who plan to be away from supply depots for months, the whole grain — which stores well in an airtight container — can be stowed in the bilge and ground into flour every now and then.

Vitamin A

Vitamin A is important to the sailor who plans a night passage because it is responsible for good night vision. It also plays a role in fighting infection, repairing body tissue, and keeping healthy skin and mucous membranes (the throat, lungs and vagina.)

"Visual purple" is a substance in the eye which is necessary for proper night vision and which is formed only in the presence of vitamin A. A small amount of it is stored in the retina of the eye, but 90% of the body's supply is stored in the liver. Under stressful conditions, the body will use up this reserve. These conditions include excessive exposure to sunlight (sunlight on water hastens the depletion), and strenuous physical activity undertaken within four hours after eating (this interferes with the absorption of vitamin A consumed at the meal, therefore calling on reserve supplies). Boaters are vulnerable to both these situations.

A single afternoon on the water without sunglasses can use up the body's reserve of vitamin A. The very painful "snow blindness" experienced by skiers is caused by improper eye protection on snow, which allows vitamin A to be leeched from the retina. A similar condition exists on the water. Boaters who say they are suffering from eye strain after a day on the water may actually be suffering from loss of vitamin A in the eye. To have sore eyes is bad enough, but to have the resulting impaired vision for night passages is far worse. Lights may be blurred or not visible from the properly safe distance. Unlit objects may not be visible until too late.

Clearly, the boater would be wise to get some vitamin A daily. Foods high in this vitamin are usually yellow, but not always: carrots (which have twice as much vitamin A when cooked), beet greens, broccoli, Swiss chard, collards, cress, endive, kale, mustard greens, parsley, red peppers, pimentos, pumpkin, spinach, squash, sweet potatoes, tomatoes, turnip greens, fortified branflakes and corn flakes, Cheddar cheese (yellow), ricotta cheese, sour cream, whipping cream, eggs, ice-cream, cow's milk, apricots, avocados, cantaloupes, sour cherries (raw), mangos, nectarines, papayas, peaches, persimmons, purple plums, prunes, watermelon, liver, liverwurst, some seafood such as crab, eel, halibut, mackerel, salmon, swordfish and whitefish, *but not* lobster, rainbow trout, frogs legs or cod (although cod liver oil is the highest known source).

Vitamin C

This is the antiscorbutic, the anti-scurvy vitamin, for lack of which entire crews sometimes perished prior to the nine-teenth century. After that time, the necessity of a constant supply of fresh fruits and vegetables was recognized. Captain Cook was the first skipper to lose not a single man to scurvy, and he achieved this feat by the revolutionary daily issuance of limes. Scurvy in general nearly disappeared around 1800, on British ships at least, because of the routine issuing lemons by the admiralty.

Death results if the body is deprived of vitamin C for prolonged periods. Sickness or malaise result if it is deprived for shorter periods. Most sailors today get some fresh fruit or vegetable every day, and scurvy is rare. However, on a long passage, minor illnesses and upsets — which may prevent you from performing at your best in an emergency — may result from inadequate intake of vitamin C. It is used up more rapidly in stress conditions. Because it is water soluble and excreted frequently in the urine, it should be supplied twice daily. The daily supply (although opinions vary widely as to just how much constitutes the minimum daily requirement) can be supplied by 1 orange, 1 green pepper, 2 onions, 1 cup of Brussels sprouts, ¼ pound liver, ¼ medium papaya, 1 cup spinach, or any number of other foods. Even 1 slice of tomato, with one tenth the recommended daily requirement, will help keep illness at bay. Dried fruits and vegetables also supply vitamin C. Most tinned fruits and vegetables supply vitamin C only if you also use the juice.

Sodium Nitrite

Many meats are cured with sodium nitrite, which is carcino-genic. Sailing without the company of sodium nitrite is difficult, but not impossible. For instance, there are a few small private companies that specialize in curing meat the old way, and a smoked ham without the chemicals will keep for years if stored in a ventilated place. Or, because sodium nitrite is water soluble, boiling first in water will rid some meats, like bacon, of most of it. Tinned bacon is very salty and the boiling also gets rid of the excessively salty flavor.

How to Dry Mushrooms

Dried mushrooms are a good shipboard item because they can dress up an otherwise dull meal. They contain good quantities of the B vitamins, potassium and phosphorus. Five pounds of fresh mushrooms when dried will pack into a 10-ounce coffee jar.

Clean mushrooms, pat them dry with tea towels or paper towels, and spread them out on a cookie tray or sheet of brown paper in a sunny spot. Turn once or twice a day for two or three days, or until they have dried and shrivelled, and rattle around when turned. Bring in at night to avoid being reconstituted by the dew. Pack into an airtight container.

Dried Orange Peel

Almost anything can be dried in this way. When gospel singer Mahalia Jackson was a child growing up in the deep South, her mother used to cut orange peels into pieces and dry them in the sun. Then in winter the dried peel was pulverized into a powder to make a tangy, vitamin C-rich drink.

How to Can Peaches

1   **cup honey, or ½ honey, ½ sugar**
2   **cups water, very hot**
1   **quart Mason jar with lid and ring**
6   **to 10 peaches, cut in halves or slices**

Stir the honey and sugar until dissolved in the hot water. Sterilize jar, lid and ring by inverting jar over 1 or 2 inches of boiling water for five minutes, keeping lid and ring beneath the water surface. Place peaches in hot jar without packing tightly, and fill jar with hot honey water to about ¾ inch from the top. Wipe rim of jar with clean towel to remove any particles that may prevent a perfect seal. Place lid on jar, then ring. Screw ring as tightly as you can by hand, then turn back ¼ turn (to allow air to escape when contents are heating). Place jar in a deep kettle filled with boiling water, so that water comes to the neck of the jar. Simmer until peaches become translucent, about 20 minutes for peach halves, a little less for slices. Remove from kettle, and immediately and gently tighten the ring. Place on counter and let cool.

How to Can Meat

Pathogenic bacteria in meat are not destroyed by the 212°F heat of the "open kettle" method described above for peaches. This is why the pressure cooker is used for meat, although I once spoke with a woman who used an oven to can meat by heating it to about 250°F.

Cut meat (beef, chicken, turtle, turkey, heart, liver, gizzard, and so on) into 1-inch cubes. Fill clean but not necessarily sterile Mason jars with the cubes to just below the neck. Fill jars with boiling water to ¾ inch from the top. Slip a knife around the edges to remove air bubbles. Place ½ teaspoon salt (which is bacteriostatic) on the top. Wipe rim of jar to remove particles. Put lid and rim in place, turning ring as tightly as you can by hand and then turning it back ¼ turn.

Place jars, 4 at a time, in the pressure cooker with a thin rack on the bottom — if jars sit right on the bottom, they may break. Put boiling water in the cooker until it comes halfway up the jars. Put lid in place. Bring to a boil and let steam escape from vent for 5 minutes, so that contents will all be at the same temperature when you start to time. Put pressure valve in place — this will be more accurate if it is a valve that shows the pounds pressure as the pressure increases. Fifteen pounds pressure, the only point that some valves (the rocker type, for instance) indicate, is not ideal for meats because it may cause some juice to be forced from the jar, perhaps impairing the seal. Turn heat down when the pressure has reached 10 pounds, and pressure cook at 10 pounds pressure for 1¼ hours. Do not handle more often than necessary, as a slight jarring movement at this point could break the seal. Let pressure come down without aid (do not place in cold water). As soon as the pressure is down, gently remove jars and retighten the ring by ¼ turn. Do not tighten any more than this or the seal may rupture. Place jars gently in an out-of-the-way spot to cool.

To can hamburger, fry it first so that it lies loosely in the jar when the water is added, allowing heat to penetrate to the center of the jar more evenly. If you use a bouillon cube in hamburger dishes, add a cube to the jar before processing. Some people add a slice of onion to the top of the jar before sealing. All these additions facilitate meal preparation on the boat and ensure a tasty supper if you should run out of condiments.

Average Diet of the Sailor Before the Nineteenth Century

(in harbor when fresh food was available)

2	**pounds of meat on 2 days**
2	**pounds of salt meat on 2 days**
¼	**pound cheese on the other 3 days**
1	**pound biscuits daily**
1	**gallon beer daily**
1	**pint of wine daily**

By the early 1800's, meat and lemon juice were issued daily.

Some Old Terms

galley down-haul — an imaginary fitting for the further confusion of a youngster his first time at seat
galley stoker — an idler
galley yarn — an empty rumor
son of a sea cook — term of abuse
grog — diluted rum
to grog — to drink
sea coal — smuggled spirits
burgoo — oatmeal porridge, from the Turkish word for wheat porridge, "burghul"
burgoo eater — a Scottish seaman
limey — an English sailor
lime juicer — an English sailing ship
bully beef — boiled salt beef
sea pork — the flesh of young whales
lobscouse — a meat and vegetable hash
lobscouser — a sailor
hard tack — ship's biscuits, baked dry before the ship left port
soft tack — ships biscuits baked en route
midshipman's nuts — broken ship's biscuits
crackerjack — dish of meat or soup mixed with broken ship's biscuits or other ingredients
manavalins — leftovers from the captain's table which were prized by others

Rum and Egg Nog

Beat an egg yolk until light. Add 1 tablespoon sugar and beat again. Add ¼ cup cream or double strength milk make from milk powder, and ¼ cup rum, and beat again. Whip the egg white until stiff and fold into the other ingredients. Various brandies can be used, too.

Hot Rum Toddy

Into a mug place 2 ounces rum, 1 teaspoon sugar or honey, and a squeeze of lemon. Fill mug with boiling water. Sprinkle with cinnamon and allspice.

Pina Colada

Mix together 1 to 2 ounces of rum with 5 to 6 ounces pineapple juice and 1 to 2 ounces coconut cream syrup (a tinned product).

PART IV
Every Which Way But East
(a log kept by Gary)

I was sitting in the Peace and Plenty Hotel in Georgetown, Exuma, sipping a luxury rum ($1.50) and gazing out at Elizabeth Harbour where a hundred or more masts rose from small ships from all over the world. The bar was filled with the crews from these cruising boats, and the sea stories were rebounding off the ancient stone walls of this once-upon-a-time slave market. The camaraderie was at a high level and the talk was divided almost equally between the forthcoming Out-Island Regatta (an annual blow-out featuring racing Bahamian work boats) and the impending migration to jobs, families and land-bound lives. Most people were looking forward to the downwind slide to Florida, with good harbors at the end of each day's run and only the caprice of the Gulf Stream to worry about before once again finding readily available beer, Burger King and bottom paint.

A new discussion flared up when I proposed heading southeast for the Turks and Caicos Islands. The skipper of a 50' motor sailor asked dubiously, "You gonna fight those trade winds in that little thing?" From another corner; "Them catamarans don't go to windward too good, do they?" and "That little six h.p. outboard all you got for power?"

This sort of "encouragement" was not what I needed, so I bowed out and turned my thoughts inward. Two weeks ago,

Dee and our aspiring deck ape, Ben (then 11½ months old), boarded a plane for Miami to take care of business there. Their trip also meant rest and recuperation from the rigors of four months cruising in a single-cabin 28' boat with a toddler. Exciting and rewarding at best ... terrifying at worst. The gray hairs were coming on faster than our precious gear disappeared over the stern. Dee arranged for a home town lad (Danny Ploeger) to fly in and join me for the trip to Caicos. She and Ben were to meet us in a month or so, reaching Providenciales in the finest up-wind rig yet devised — the commercial airliner.

Our dream is to homestead on North Caicos on a plot of land where *Mariposa* can bob on a mooring in a safe anchorage and we can gaze out to open sea as we hoe potatoes under the tropical sun. Years of island cruising have brought us to the realization that this is what we want. A base, far from the maddening crowd, a simple life in a less complex society. Idealistic and somewhat naïve, some might say, but we have to try it at least.

Danny appeared at four o'clock, right on schedule, dragging two huge cartons of "contraband" in addition to his knapsack. He had been up for three days straight, and had been grilled by customs and immigration at three borders. He looked like the lone survivor of a shipwreck and mumbled incoherently of the indignities of modern public transport. I plied him with rum and sympathy. Dee had intercepted him at Miami International Airport and loaded him down with over a hundred pounds of supplies. Wow! Unheard of goodies! A beautiful new "Big Ben" type ship's chronometer, Cuban sausage, sunglasses, granola bars, and even a huge cooked turkey, complete with stuffing and cranberry sauce. Just like Christmas! Injections of peanut butter, ketchup, pipe tobacco, and yes, real fresh green money! Superb planning! That Dee really knows how to do it! She may not be with us in body, but in spirit, she's right here! I must keep this log of the trip if only for her eyes.

We played around Georgetown for a few days, falling off sailboards, diving, and waiting for the mailboat to come in with fresh eggs and our lost mail from Great Inagua (ho-ho). We met some people from Germany who had brushed with a reef in a 40' C&C and they were shepherding back to Miami for an owner in Hamburg. Nice kids, interested in acquiring a big tri and going into the charter business in the Bahamas. They had several young Fräuleins on board who insisted on skinny dipping every morning, and of course Danny fell in love with each one of them; a different one every day.

Our plan for gaining easting safely was to turn this voyage into a series of day sails. By waiting for favorable winds that would allow us to lay a direct course each day, I felt we could avoid the hazards of night sailing in these unpredictable waters. Seven or eight good sailing days, with the wind off the nose, is all we asked.

April 10, 1980. The mailboat arrived, but no mail. We decided to leave before Danny got himself into a compromising situation. I told him that the sea would cleanse his mind of unholy thoughts. We left on light easterly winds and beat our way down to Hog Cay Cut. Really fine sailing, albeit a little on the nose.

We caught a 12-pound mutton snapper by trolling with the skin from one of his lost kinfolk, dried from a previous day of fishing. This, by the way, is one way to cut down on the cost of lures. Just take the skin from any fish you catch and hang it to dry in the sun. Then when you want to fish, just cut off a chunk and fasten it on an old lure that has lost all its feathers, or to a bare hook with a weight to carry it down a bit.

We lost a few prospects at first because the piece of bait was too long and the fish would strike, shred the bait and miss the hook. Fat city! We ate snapper for the next two days and even dried some for fishcakes later. Danny would wince and run his belly when I threatened to bait a new hook.

We ran aground going through Hog Cay Cut, still high on our fishing success — a classic example of euphoria and bad light. But we got off easily, and put down our anchor for the night.

April 11, 1980. The winds were easterly to east-north-easterly this morning, so we decided to set a course for the south end of Long Island. We left with all sail up on a beam reach. Nice sailing. We must have experienced some currents, as we made landfall downwind of our course and had to tack to clear Neuvitas Rocks. But we passed through with no bad moments, proceeding to Galloway Landing where we anchored in 9 feet of water over a white sand bottom, one ama almost on shore.

Danny experienced "mal de mer" when he went below to cook lunch and retired to his bunk for the rest of the day: something about the combination of alcohol fumes, frying food and a surge at anchor. He revived, however, in time for a supper of fried leftover potatoes, green peppers and onions, with Cuban sausage on the side.

April 12, 1980. Today we sped down the west coast of Long Island at ten knots in winds of 15 to 20 knots and negligible sea condition. As we reached closer to the "horn," this being the extreme southerly tip of the island, we began to bounce. According to the *West Indies Pilot*, this spot is known for freak waves caused by 2 knot northeast setting current meeting shoaling water and the prevailing easterly winds.

It lived up to its reputation. We discovered all the weak points in our stowage system. Various containers came loose and leapt around the cabin. Luckily we had already reefed the genoa and tied a longer painter on the dinghy. I kept kicking myself for not bringing the dinghy on board before departing. Hindsight is 20/20. We gave the south coast a 5-mile offing and rounded up for our beat to Little Harbour, ten miles up the coast.

By this point Danny was glued to the bunk and couldn't function except under extreme duress. He has a game attitude towards seasickness but is still learning to take the "pill" *before* we leave harbor. The seas were quite out of proportion to the wind strength today, some of them over 10 feet, and breaking in gusts — perhaps the product of a disturbance in northern waters. They blew three sides out of the main and I had to take it down for fear of more damage. This made it hard to beat our way north to Little Harbour, especially approaching from the south with no good landmarks and the ingrained reluctance to close with a lee shore.

We entered with the dinghy trying to ram its way through the transom and waves breaking in great orgies of spray to the right and left of us . . . and, now and then, right where we were heading. You have to head through somewhere, right? Anyway, tonight, we are sitting pretty in this fine harbor, with the waves crashing at the entrance and that fat feeling of being safe and "smart."

Tomorrow, we'll fix the mainsail, make a few adjustments, and wait for the seas to go down a bit before the beat across Crooked Island Passage.

We ended up spending five days in Little Harbour and ran into the Deans (a local native family) again. Mitchell, now 18 years old, came out to the boat and was very surprised and pleased to see us. He still remembered his first taste of pizza, thanks to Dee on our 1975 trip. Mitch was shocked to hear of *Isla's* end. He kept saying, "That beautiful boat!"

We visited their home in the village of Roses, a typically quaint out-island settlement with pink, turquoise and baby blue houses and a school with all the children in smart brown and white uniforms. The farming here is of the slash and burn type. Very effective for one year, but it leeches all nutrients out of the soil and the plot has to be moved the following year. Goats, chickens and pigs able about, idly gleaning subsistence from this arid land. The ground is 90 per cent rock, but the little deposits of soil bloom with all manner of flora at the slightest hint of rain. Mitch says that a heavy dew will get seeds sprouting. He and his parents entered into a pact to keep us there and buy land. It's tempting, but we still have our love affair with Caicos. Mitch is into guitars and drums, and has his own band that plays at weddings and dances. He and Danny turned out to be real soul brothers. They spent hours with their guitars and tape recorders. Danny says he wants to come down here and stay for six months. Mitch says that if he does, he must stay with them.

There is a real winter norther blowing, with winds shifting from south to north and gusting up to 35 knots. What ever happened to west winds?

We're still living like kings on all the goodies Dee sent us. I'm trying to ration them. Little Harbour seems to be all conched and fished out. It is too rough to go fishing on the outer reef.

April 17, 1980. It is now 1600 hours. I am sipping a rum and licking my wounds. Danny is comatose in his bunk. We departed this morning at 0900 on the tide and headed for Crooked Island. We left under reefed main. The wind was just forward of the beam, the seas just behind. Some of the seas were monstrous, but the wind was fair and we were laying course. Danny commented on the size of the seas and I assured him that they would be much smaller as soon as we reached deeper water. Not so. They actually built as we got further offshore and became confused as the wind veered more easterly.

At 1100 I decided to raise the reefed genny for speed and pointing ability. This seemed to give us too much speed and we leapt forward, ramming through the waves rather than up and over them. That would not do. So I dropped the main and the pin at the bottom of the track, decided to let go. The whole sail started beating a tattoo on the deck. About that time, the genny shackle parted, leaving the genny flogging and the halyard swinging in great circles and heading for the mast head. Seas were breaking all around us and catching us in some rather embarrassing positions, so we started the outboard and held her into the wind as best we could. After long minutes of modern ballet on the cabin top, I managed to capture the genny halyard and tie a bowline (best sail attachment yet) in its head.

With the motor running and the genny up, we appeared to have fair control. Not for long. The wind veered another 20 degrees and we found ourselves heading on a course so southerly that we could not expect to close with land before darkness. We were then close-hauled in large quartering seas! Leaving Danny on the helm (with his "mal de mer" and his lack of knowledge of what a huge breaking beam wave can do to a small multihull), I struggled forward to put a second reef in the main, hoping with this maneuvre to again lay course and avoid the biggest waves. Somehow, the main sheet had tied itself in a knot and after several unsuccessful attempts at sorting it out and many near broaches, I gave up. I put down the helm and headed, tail between my legs, for the shelter of Long Island.

Danny found this new motion even harder on his system and retired below. I seemed to be doing a lot more single-handing all of a sudden! We slid under the end of the island in only two hours and found a lee anchorage: much relief at arriving alive, and some despair as I calculated our "easting." So much for the lucky feeling when I woke up this morning and realized Ben had entered this world just one year ago today. I miss him right now, and his mother, too. Wish you wuz here!

April 19, 1980. We sat around yesterday feeling sorry for ourselves. Going into the village of Mortimers for water, we found the situation bad. all of the Bahamas have suffered from drought this year. Salt Pond on Long Island had zero inches of rainfall! One kindly old fellow did offer us some brownish liquid, which we took for emergencies.

There is a 40' fishing smack anchored here, also waiting out the weather.

Saw a ten-foot shark checking out our boat. Didn't go swimming.

Awoke this morning to find the winds easterly and light.

We decided to head out anyway. At least the seas were down some. We motored around the point and saw the smack heading out, too. We cheated and motor-sailed so that we could point higher. The wind soon picked up and we raised the full main and reefed genny. The seas were still big but at least not breaking. With an overloaded boat and untried rig one tends to be cautious. We fell off one big wave and ripped the clew cringle out of the main — should have been reinforced back in harbor. I never learn! We were able to jury-rig it by passing lines through the bottom batten-tie grommets. I never use that full batten anyway. It makes for a somewhat baggy set to the sail, but better than reefing. Danny took his pill and his stomach held up fine today. He even thought the big waves were sort of fun.

After 12 hours on the same tack, with the winds gradually backing, we entered the "harbor" (3 knots of current and no protection from the east) behind Windsor Point on Crooked Island. The water was over ten feet deep right up to shore and the land was covered with trees and plants of every color — more beautiful than most manicured parks. It was another rocky-rolly anchorage, but we slept like logs. Cuban sausage and dried lima beans, and mung bean sprouts for supper.

April 20, 1980. Overcast and threatening again today for the third day in a row. As usual on Sunday mornings, I can't get a weather forecast. Just trust in the Lord and raise the sails, I guess. We set sail for Landrail Point, just below Bird Rock Light on the northwest end of Crooked.

The winds blew weakly from all points of the compass, so we drifted, motored and occasionally sailed our way to our destination. There were three other cruising boats there, rolling miserably in the surge. A couple of hedas poked up and hands fluttered listlessly in greeting as we ghosted into the harbor. At noon I got a U.S. weather forecast that called for a low moving eastward, and westerly winds. We decided to head across the north end of Crooked and see how far we could get before nightfall.

We caught a four-foot barracuda just north of Bird Rock, but let him go when we saw his eyes. He looked sick. Fish poisoning we do not need! There's lots of traffic here; six ships passed us today and three yesterday. One that was on a collision course with us made a drastic course change to miss us and even did it early enough to save me some gray hairs. I wondered if the watch officer was also a small boat sailor.

We had no sooner gotten a few miles offing than the winds came around out of the north and strengthened. Sure, sure, I thought, here we are on the north shore of a reef-bound island with a norther starting, contrary to all reports! Our fears were shortlived, however, as the winds finally dropped to nothing and we had to motor into Major's Cay Harbour, about halfway across the island. So, we were 20 miles farther east than if we'd stayed at Bird Rock. Nicer anchorage too. Good light required to enter here — a true barrier reef, with only small breaks here and there. The inner harbor even had coral heads, reaching out like grasping fingers for the unwary ship. Two anchors tonight!

I guess the gas situation is pretty bad everywhere. We were approached by a sport fisherman today who boomed at us through his megaphone, "Is there any place within 30 miles I can get fuel?" We shouted back, "Not to our knowledge," and he wallowed wearily away in a westerly direction. It must be scary to be in a ship that will not function without fuel when sources are so few and far between.

We hope to buy 5 gallons for ourselves at Atwood Harbour. We may have problems other than gas, as I forgot to get bills changed back at Georgetown. As a result, I look like the proverbial yachtsman, or even worse, a successful drug runner with only hundred dollar bills in my pocket. Some of these people have never even seen a hundred dollar bill. Not too swift, Hodgkins! Danny just produced a handful of multi-colored Canadian bills — don't think they'll take that. Oh well, we're a sailing vessel, right? Right!

April 21, 1980. Today was filled with every kind of sailing imaginable. We picked our way out through the reef with light southerly winds, the sky ominous with huge thunderheads, and bordering showers spitting on us already. Clear of the reefs, we turned east. One minute we would be ghosting along at less than a knot, the next, roaring forward, holding the genny sheet in white knuckles at ten knots plus. First, the sun would shine brightly, then we would be inundated with driving rain, at times completely obscuring the reef and Acklins Island, just a couple of miles to the south.

This mammoth low pressure system has been a real gift to us. It provided winds from the south, southeast, west and northwest, all good for us, and scarce in the region. As we approached Atwood, a huge squall moved in and turned visibility to zero. Just as we decided to head back out to sea it cleared and we entered the harbor in bright sunlight. What a day!

I even managed to bake a loaf of whole-wheat-soy-oat bread while underway. I've been making yeast bread every few days and almost know how by now. Danny is easy to feed, he will eat anything that doesn't eat him first. He is also into really nutritious foods and is as wild as I am about sprouts, whole grains, and so on. Lucky. Dee did a fantastic job of provisioning Mariposa. We could live for a year on the dried foods in the bilges.

We went beachcombing and found the wreckage of a powerboat and a beautifully built old sailing hull. We also found a like-new toilet brush, identical to the one Ben dropped over at Georgetown. Lots of nice shells here, too. Danny found a small conch shell (about 4 inches) delicately etched in browns, blacks and beiges, one of the prettiest I've ever seen. I gathered some sunrise tellins for Dee's collection. No settlement here, just a fisherman's house on the west side of the harbor. I hope to find some fresh water before we leave.

At about 1600 hours, the wind came up from the northwest (our only unprotected direction) and blew like stink all night. Even at anchor, it felt like we were doing 10 knots. But there's a hard sand bottom and good scope on our anchors. All of our clothes that got soaked yesterday are now drying out — the inside of the cabin looks like a laundry.

April 22, 1980. Neither of us slept much last night. The winds kept at it, so anchor checks were regular. At 0630 hours we started fishing for a weather forecast. Finally caught one out of Cape Haitien at 0715 on station 4VEH. It didn't tell us much. The present wind is a perfect direction from Mayaguana, but we first have to beat out of the harbor in a north-northwesterly direction, where we would be embayed by the reef until we were 3 or 4 miles off. What a quandary. The right wind, but we can't get out to use it. A big four-banger diesel would be nice right now! Seems there is a gale just north of us with winds over 40 knots and seas over 15 feet. Moderating seas are expected tonight and tomorrow, so I think we'll wait. Florida weather says they have northerly winds at 10 to 15 knots. Tomorrow looks like the day to move.

Danny is a real tea granny, and we seem to be out of tea. Poor Danny — no beer, no cigarettes, and now — horrors — no tea! He'll be a monk by the time he gets home.

After lunch we decided to row ashore and walk around the bay to the narrow creek at the southwest end of the harbor. We thought it might be a good hurricane hole for future use. The sky was clear, the wind howling, a real high pressure day. Any fool could see that the rain squalls were over. We luxuriated in the clean white sand squeezing between our toes and the hot sun, moderated by wind, shining down on us. Nothing like a brisk walk after the relative inactivity of shipboard life. We cast glances back at *Mariposa*, a jewel in the golden sunlight, set in turquoise water, her hatches and ports open to the drying breeze.

Suddenly, Danny wheeled and pointed out to sea and said, "What's that?" Less than a mile away there was a horrendous black cloud, spewing froth buckets of water heading relentlessly for our poor little vessel. We shot off at full gallop, man against nature — a battle of wills! After the first quarter mile, Danny's 22-year-old body was just getting in stride. My 39-year-old model was beginning to feel that sleeping in a wet bunk wasn't really that bad. The squall hit with unbridled fury, inundating us. We finally reached the *Mariposa* in the half swamped dinghy, leapt aboard and slammed all ports shut. As we crept below into the soggy interior and dogged down the main companion, the rain stopped and I glimpsed blue sky under the black veil and old man sun grinning sardonically.

April 23, 1980. This morning we found the winds still from a northerly direction, but moderated. We headed out to sea at 0630 hours, engine cavitating wildly, and just made it through the steep waves at the entrance. There is no need to feel guilty for not leaving yesterday. We could not have made it through the rollers that were pounding in then. Down to two gallons of water, it is now imperative that we get to Mayaguana and stock up.

By mid-morning, we were running short of wind and changed to the drifter. The rest of the day was spent going from almost dead calm to surging along in big seas at 6 to 8 knots. Didn't sight Mayaguana until 1700 and realized it was going to be a night entrance, our first of the voyage. Luckily, we had a half moon and clear skies. We sorted our way nervously into Start Bay under moonlight, just rounding below the breaking reef — ghostly shapes of white water growling threateningly at us. We kept trying to get our anchor down as soon as we rounded the end of the island, but even though we could see the bottom, 60 feet of chain and anchor just rode straight down. We finally grabbed bottom in 25 feet of water, only 50 yards off shore.

We fell gratefully into our bunks, still doubting whether we were actually where we thought we were. Moonlight landfalls — argggh!

April 24, 1980. Great day! We were where we thought we were! And now we were faced with a fifteen-mile beat to Abraham's Bay, but the island gave us a lee and smooth water. The winds were up and down as usual. It was fun going to windward in these conditions.

Around noon, just off the abandoned missile station, our clothespin snapped on the trolling line and we looked back to see a rainbow flash break the surface, 250 feet behind us. A dorado! I handed Danny the helm and started hauling him in. We landed him, and he was a beauty, about 25 pounds. He leapt madly about the cockpit, almost knocking us overboard and covering everything in scales. I couldn't believe we had finally gotten a dorado on board. We've hooked so many of these beautiful fighters over the years, and lost *all* of them. Danny's exclamation just about summed it up. "Hot damn, what a fish!"

We spied a 30' monohull, belly-up on the reef, and found out later from the natives that the owner of it had lost *three* boats to coral reefs. He's either awfully unlucky, or awfully stupid. We anchored at Abraham's Bay at 1300 hours. Needless to say, fish was for lunch.

Oh, my aching back! We went into town to get water, and had to carry our 5 gallon jugs over a mile. Had a beer each at $1.25 a piece; bought white flour at $1.85 for 5 pounds; and ten tea bags for $1.15 — from three different stores.

We gave some of our huge fish to a lady on shore. She was amazed. "You givin' it away, mon?"

The water had to be bucketed out of a communal well at the village center, and Danny lost the bucket down the well, much to the glee of a dozen or more youngsters who had gathered to see these white men. One little girl was being urged forward by her older sister to meet us. She crept shyly closer, then suddenly turned and fled, crying, "I's scared, I's scared!" Several of the older girls were eyeing Danny's long, blond, almost white curls as if they would like to run their fingers through them — such a contrast. One guy ran home and got us a meat hook. With this and some line we were able to recover the bucket and some of our dignity.

There was a new phone station here and we tried to put a call through, but something was out of order. Maybe the next day, if we were still here. It's a pretty little town. Not many tourists stop by. There are two goats in every front yard and a pig fattening out behind. Since the missile station closed down 15 years ago, there is little paid employment for the men, but they are ardent fishermen. All day they have been coming in loaded down with conch to be shipped to the Nassau market.

Back in the harbor, we met the people on a 26' cat, *Another Rainbow Chaser.* They had just crossed the Atlantic and were taking the boat to Florida. They invited us over for drinks, and we tried to lay some fish on them. "Oh no," said they, "we just bought 6 pounds of lobster tails from the fishermen." It turns out that they are from Sudbury, Ontario and have a summer place on Manitoulin Island. They also have a 30' Piver that is in need of tender loving care. Danny really got excited! He also has been living on Manitoulin Island and wants a boat. After many Mount Gay rums and a belly full of lobster, some kind of tentative deal was worked out. Seems Danny could have the boat for the price of the rig. What a deal! With his skill at cabinet and guitar making, it should be a breeze for him. Suddenly he was anxious to get home. This is boat-building weather in Canada. He said he'd see me through to Caicos, though.

All that lobster, on top of all that fish — I'm glad we didn't have to swim home. We stumbled into bed and slept like the dead.

April 25, 1980. Winds from the southeast this morning, which was our course to Caicos. So we had to stay. This layover continued to be charmed — our magic place. When I went ashore and phoned Miami, I didn't expect Dee to be there, but I thought I could leave a message that we still lived and were approaching our destination. After half an hour of static and calling for the Nassau mobile operator, I had just about given up hope. Then, just as we were poised to leave, the man at the set said, "Take it in the booth, I got your lady on the line." Great to hear Dee's voice, I was totally flustered and unable to gather my thoughts, as I really hadn't expected to get her. She was in good spirits and howled with approval when I told her of our progress. Ben was howling too, she said, but not for my benefit.

Dee's big news was that she had reached the PRIDE organization and had been hired for lab research on Pine Cay, only eight miles from North Caicos. What a break for us! This would give us time to look around without that terrible urgency and desperation that I, at least, would feel if we hadn't anything else going for us. I knew, too, that Dee gets a real thrill out of the work. She is an ardent researcher at all times. She has scribblers filled with far-flung bits of information and wisdom on a million different topics. She calls them her "everything books." PRIDE is doing conch research and solar and wind energy projects, areas of great interest to both of us. Dee says that she and Ben will be flying into Providenciales on May 7.

As I write this, it is April 27 and the wind is still whistling out of the southeast. I hope to get out of here tomorrow.

April 29, 1980. Today is Danny's birthday, and we have already demolished the caramel cake I made him yesterday. It was good, but sooo sweet! Quite a change from our normal diet.

I discovered that we were on daylight saving time, so our planned 0530 rising was actually 0430 by our biological clocks. Somehow, we managed to leave at first light. The winds were south-south-westerly and light, and we were making 3 to 4 knots under drifter and main. We needed to average 5 knots to guarantee a daylight landfall at West Caicos. As the day progressed it was questionable whether we would make it. The wind died, veered, backed, and died again. We made 5 knots under power for an hour and a half, but we could not continue as the fuel was just a gallon or so.

Late in the afternoon, the squalls started marching toward us, filling us with knot-in-the-stomach apprehension. Would we get there before dark? Was that a reef ahead through the blackness of the storm, or just a breaking wave? Always something to keep us on edge. With the squalls came wind — we would speed up to 6 or 8 knots with each one — little spurts of power propelling us towards our landfall.

Around 1500, between squalls, we sighted the northwest point of Provo and felt somewhat relieved. At least an accurate position check was possible. With the wind backing, we knew we'd have trouble making it in before dark, and with that overcast, our much coveted full moon would do us no good. I didn't like the way things were going at all — no lighthouses, and too may reefs. Dicey!

We spied two fishermen working the reef and decided to ask them if there was a short cut to Sand Bore Channel. We picked our way through the coral heads until we were close enough to hail them. They informed us that there was a way, and we should follow them. They eventually led us right up onto a shoal, and there we sat, with night coming on and dubious weather all around. The fisherman at the helm introduced himself as Henry and said encouragingly, "Don't worry, mon, we pull you off." The other fisherman said nothing, just smiled knowingly and continued skinning the conch that swirled in a slimy mass at his feet. He was gloriously attired in a slouch hat, "it's-better-in-the-Bahamas" T-shirt and polka dot cut-offs.

I tossed Henry a line, and sure enough, with his six h.p. outboard pulling and ours pushing, we floated free. Then the fire drill really started. I didn't get the line uncleated in time — *Mariposa* surged forward under full power — Danny didn't throttle back soon enough — Henry couldn't get his end of the towline, as he had tied a knot and it was under tension. The line took up and brought them careening into the side of our ama. What a fiasco! Henry's buddy was unruffled by all of this, and didn't miss a stroke in his skinning. Henry grinned slyly. "You been here before?" (Danny trying to fend their fishing hull off our shiny topsides.) "Yah, mon, I remembers you, you in dat dark boat, dat big one. Yah, Yah, I knows you. You Gary, right?" Amazing, he did know me, and remembered from 3 years ago. What a memory! These people are something else.

They putted off, smiling and waving. I shouted after them that I would stand them a beer when we got in. Be damned if I can remember Henry!

We anchored in the dark at Gussy Point. With the beat over, I felt that it wasn't really all that bad.

C'mon Dee, c'mon Ben, let's get started!

Index of Recipes and Foods

One-pot Meals

Seafood

Other Meals

Vegetables

Desserts

Breakfast

Flotsam and Jetsam